T0248181

BURNT OUT

TO

LIT UP

DAISY AUGER-DOMÍNGUEZ

BURNT OUT

TO

LIT UP

HOW TO **REIGNITE** THE **JOY** OF **LEADING PEOPLE**

WILEY

Published by John Wiley & Sons, Inc., Hoboken, New Jersey.

Published simultaneously in Canada.

For general information on our other products and services or for technical support, please contact our Customer Care Department within the United States at (800) 762-2974, outside the United States at (317) 572-3993 or fax (317) 572-4002.

Wiley also publishes its books in a variety of electronic formats. Some content that appears in print may not be available in electronic formats. For more information about Wiley products, visit our web site at www.wiley.com.

Library of Congress Cataloging-in-Publication Data

Names: Auger-Domínguez, Daisy, author.
Title: Burnt out to lit up : how to reignite the joy of leading people / Daisy Auger-Domínguez.
Description: Hoboken, New Jersey : Wiley, [2024] | Includes bibliographical references and index.
Identifiers: LCCN 2024006716 (print) | LCCN 2024006717 (ebook) | ISBN 9781394254293 (cloth) | ISBN 9781394254316 (adobe pdf) | ISBN 9781394254309 (epub)
Subjects: LCSH: Management—Psychological aspects. | Leadership—Psychological aspects. | Burn out (Psychology) | Job satisfaction.
Classification: LCC HD31.2 .A94 2024 (print) | LCC HD31.2 (ebook) | DDC 658.4/092—dc23/eng/20240530
LC record available at https://lccn.loc.gov/2024006716
LC ebook record available at https://lccn.loc.gov/2024006717

Cover Design: Paul McCarthy
Cover Image: © Getty Images | Seth Joel

SKY10085818_092424

To the managers committed to turning their burnout into light

Contents

Introduction

I remember when I loved my job, enjoyed going to work, and delighted in helping people through tough, strange, and rewarding experiences. But leading people while on the brink of burnout? Well that's a whole other story.

On Monday, July 10, 2023, I was wrapping up emails before going to bed and came across an update from our communications team addressed to me, our co-CEOs, and legal counsel. It referred to the cash compensation of senior executives over the past year, disclosed in our Chapter 11 bankruptcy submission. We were warned of the onslaught of inevitable negative responses.

The email said, "People are talking."

I didn't dwell on it. Our bankruptcy process had been tumultuous, with information leaking from every conceivable source, accurate or not. This was, I figured, just another chapter in our messy story.

As I was transitioning from my role as Chief People Officer at Vice during its headline-grabbing bankruptcy process, my days were consumed with helping our team secure severance payments for laid-off employees—an issue that the bankruptcy courts had blocked for months. Facing the emotional toll and uncertainty this process had on employees was grueling for everyone, myself included. Vice's public image took a backseat in my mind, and I was primarily concerned with the way these choices were impacting the employees I'd supported for three years.

However, following that email, a colleague told us that one of our journalists had turned to then-named-Twitter to reveal the salaries and bonuses of senior executives, including me, framing the amounts as a symbol of Vice's declining moral and financial condition.

I read the tweet and sighed. I had grown desensitized to the ongoing drama.

Before going to sleep, I casually told my husband that our salaries had been leaked, shaking my head and saying, "I'll deal with this tomorrow." It was frustrating to have my private information exposed, but in the grand scheme of things, it was out in the open for everyone to see. Leaks had become synonymous with Vice.

The following morning, I woke up early and headed to the gym, checking my email during my subway ride, finding nothing of note. My daughter was away at camp, and my husband worked from home that day. It was another workday, with the hope of getting closer to solving a recurring task: sorting out the latest severance payment challenge.

However, I had yet to check social media.

As I rode the subway back home, my inbox flooded with emails from our co-CEOs asking, "What should we do about this?"

Uncertain, I began by examining social media, then delved into the hundreds of responses from the employee tweet.

My heart stopped.

Sure, there were tweets, but that was just the beginning.

My inbox and DMs became inundated with comments like "fuck off you hack" and demands to "pay people you worthless piece of shit."

I had been trapped in a daily grind for months, executing painful layoffs while holding people through the aftermath of bankruptcy and battling to secure severance payments for laid-off employees. The mockery and contempt aimed at my compensation were misplaced and infuriating.

"¡Coño!"

I—someone who had spent my career building inclusive and equitable workplaces—was portrayed as heartlessly laying off hundreds of employees while pocketing extravagant bonuses.

Now, this wasn't my first "Rising Above the Challenges: A Workplace Story." As a Latina who defied the odds to rise to the executive ranks of some of the world's most admired companies, I've often felt overlooked for my contributions and subjected to unwarranted scrutiny. I've been tasked with cleaning up the messes left behind by others, all while facing pressure to conform, downplay, and mute who I was.

I've also endured hurtful messages from colleagues, managers, and even right-wing extremists questioning my worth. In my senior leadership human resources role, I was often the go-between at the intersection of employees and leaders. Leader complaints and fears came to me. What employees couldn't say directly to their managers or company leaders, they would say to me. I was the sounding board, and sometimes the punching bag—it came with the territory.

But this time was different. I was the target of a smear campaign, painted as a greedy, unethical executive.

Being the target of mobs who loathed *me,* instead of those responsible for this mess, was hard. Didn't they know that I was just as fed up with this flawed system as they were?

I felt like I had been punched in the gut.

After years of guiding other people through organizational fires, I was the one who got burned. And one step closer to being burned out. Like, burnt crispy.

But here's the thing.

As much as I wanted to throw up my hands and say "I quit!", by staying and immersing myself in the discomfort and chaos, I met the leader I was destined to be.

As I made my way through the turmoil, I discovered the power within to lead people in the way I was truly meant to.

That's why I want to help others, especially those entrusted with managing people, to free themselves from the weight of burnout, unending demands, tension, and chaos so that they may radiate a brighter light for others. (And feel good about themselves too!)

While the relentless attacks hurt, I sought refuge in others and opened myself up to the help that was generously offered. My husband's steadfast love extended to managing my social media feeds and ensuring I didn't skip meals. Reassuring texts appeared out of the blue, like the one from a friend, a high-profile white male attorney, who wrote, "No need for apologies. A white man wouldn't apologize. You are worth every penny, and HR is not accountable for financial decisions."

I knew this, but it was hard to embrace amid the noise. The questions gnawed at me: Would these allegations tarnish my reputation? Would I be shunned by colleagues or future employers? When would this end?

I turned to a communications crisis expert, who stressed the value of keeping a steady composure. Everyone was racing to say or report anything that would keep the drama alive. It felt like a twisted reality show where everyone wanted their moment in the spotlight. The time for telling my story would come, but for now, I needed space and time to unfold.

I knew this was the way to go. I'd doled out this counsel to dozens of leaders, mostly white men, over the years. But when you find yourself in the thick of such loathsome hostility, what you hunger for most is a healthy dose of grace.

Occasional moments of relief reminded me that this, too, would pass. However, sporadic texts from friends like "Are you holding up alright? I came across this. . ." swiftly reignited the anguish. "Ay, Daisy, take a deep breath. Come back to yourself," I would tell myself.

I confronted the daily fury that became my shadow during the most demanding years of leading people as the top HR executive of a global media company. Over three grueling years, my role involved navigating our workforce through an unprecedented triad of crises—health, economic, and societal upheavals. Executing cost-saving layoffs while ensuring the respect and dignity of each impacted human intensified my sense of injustice. That summer, my heart went out to those who suffered because of our company's bankruptcy, and the burden of guilt was overwhelming because I couldn't change their circumstances.

I couldn't shoulder that heavy load indefinitely. No one should.

Through the firestorm, I continued to do my job, advocating for employees and supporting my team, leaders, and managers through this latest crisis. I doubled down on empathy and compassion and became a one-woman persuasion machine for the rights of employees to voice their concerns. Despite weathering unfair personal attacks, I upheld my commitment to treating every employee with dignity and respect.

I know the feeling all too well—being engulfed by chaos and yet pressing on. And here's what I've learned: As a leader, when you find yourself amid a raging fire without a clear escape route, you have no choice but to take that first step and lead yourself and your teams through the flames.

Here We Go

According to conventional wisdom, leaders are the architects of an organization's overall tone, vision, and strategy, while managers transform these high-level ideas into practical steps. Both roles lead people, but managers are key in advancing tasks, initiatives, and products. Their effectiveness hinges on their ability to nurture their team's talents, experiences, and well-being to meet goals.

Leaders and Managers

This book is dedicated to leaders who manage people in *every* aspect, bearing a significant share of responsibilities. Throughout the book, I'll use "manager" as shorthand, emphasizing that in the modern workplace, the essence of management is fundamentally about leading people.

Everyone wants to manage people until they have to manage people. That's my cheeky advice to those itching for leadership promotions before they're ready.

Managers are in the trenches, day in and day out, with the most direct influence on how their teams experience the workplace, produce, and perform. When it comes to transforming an organization, the spotlight shines on the managers. They can play a part in creating either burnout-inducing work environments or nurturing spaces where employees thrive and find fulfillment and joy in their roles.

Great managers are more than just team leaders tasked with delivering results; they're the fuel that drives motivation, commitment, and the perception of leadership within a company. Their influence stretches beyond their immediate team, shaping the organizational culture and instilling external confidence.

While you probably won't find these specifics listed in the standard job requirements and qualifications section of a typical job description, here's my take on the modern "must haves" for managers:

1. Strong sense of accountability and transparency, able to oversee both the well-being and productivity of teams
2. Excellent collaboration and communication skills with their teams, senior leadership, the public, peers, partners, vendors, investors, clients, and customers
3. Advanced diversity and inclusion skills, including demonstrated ability to increase racial representation; to inspire teams to rise above cancel culture, outdated organizational norms, social media backlash, and polarization; and to adjust practices to avoid backlash from stakeholders including employees, customers, boards, and investors

4. Strong understanding of how global social and economic upheaval impacts brands, external relationships, internal culture, project timelines, budgets, financial performance, and stock market performance

5. Ability to understand people in all of their complexity and advocate for their identities, values, and beliefs while rallying to a shared vision

6. Proficiency in decision-making, taking calculated risks and cultivating an environment that encourages innovative and creative thinking and embraces unconventional, forward-looking ideas where failure is seen as an opportunity for learning and growth—while managing leaders clinging to the status quo

7. Ability to convey conviction and confidence while leading meetings and engaging in conversations, especially during turbulent social change, without causing offense, hurt, or alienation

8. Resilience in coaching and guiding teams through professional and personal challenges, consistently motivating them to achieve peak performance, even in the aftermath of crises, major restructurings, layoffs, or mergers

9. Capacity to serve as a bridge and a facilitator between various stakeholders

Can you relate to any of these? I've seen how these ever-increasing and perplexing responsibilities can drain even the most well-intentioned and capable managers. I want to help you steer clear of the burnout trap.

Who Makes a Good Manager?

Well, it's a bit like you know it when you see it. Good managers, like Hamilton's immigrants, "get the job done," but *not* at the expense of their team members. They listen, communicate, and advocate for their teams. They get the big picture, the "why," and how it feeds into their team's contributions. They lend an ear to their team's concerns and uncertainties, cultivating trust and shared understanding and promoting collaborative problem-solving instead of playing the "blame game."

Good management enables trust, outstanding performance, and a positive experience, rather than entitling lousy behavior.

Earning trust can be tricky when you lack information. Good managers communicate expectations clearly, guide their teams to understand what's important—priorities—rather than just handing out tasks, and consistently assess what's going well and what needs improvement.

When you manage well, you free yourself up to do your best solo work. But you have to put in the time.

Management is like a high-wire act of care, where you continually juggle decisions about schedules, tasks, demands, unforeseen circumstances, commitments, and, always, humans. One misstep can disrupt the performance.

What's the fallout of a managerial misstep? A manager lacking confidence might shy away from providing constructive feedback needed for an employee's development and the successful completion of a project. Another manager lacking organizational acumen or strong relationships might fail to discern market or organizational signals, resulting in unprepared teams when facing strategic shifts in product launches or project deadlines. A manager grappling with fear about their own position may struggle to make sound decisions or offer clear guidance and possibly react in a way that causes distress and confusion among the team.

> *"I want to be a manager when I grow up,"* said no one.

Not many people aspired to be managers when they were kids. But for many of us, becoming a manager seemed like the only path to higher leadership levels—am I right? While some may see management roles as a way to boost their egos or advance their careers, the new workplace makes it difficult to achieve either. In my experience, management is a challenging and humbling role filled with moments that require us to tap into the deepest reserves of our humanity.

Managers are expected to be superheroes. They must hold people together; navigate intricate interpersonal, political, and legal challenges; and address issues like sudden downsizing, layoffs, leadership transitions, and, as I've personally experienced, even bankruptcy. These shifts can leave employees feeling abandoned and uncertain, putting tremendous pressure on managers to hold it all together.

Leading people has become a nearly impossible job. A handful of employee and operational issues can easily hijack your entire week, diverting your attention from your previous priorities and wreaking havoc on your efforts to reprioritize tasks and manage the overload for your teams.

But not all managers get it right, and leading people when frequently buried under a mountain of tasks and left without the support they need is stressing everyone out. Employees suffer—and, ultimately, so do company results and shareholders.

I've witnessed the damage caused by disengaged and neglectful managers and how employees can thrive under the guidance of caring managers who help navigate personal, interpersonal, and organizational challenges.

Far too often, I've seen highly talented individuals, some genuinely well-intentioned, thrust into management roles without adequate preparation, organizational perspective, or self-awareness. Essentially, they are left to learn on the job. While a few may have an innate aptitude for leading people, most are left to their own devices, with management essentially hoping for the best. If they're lucky, they have good role models to emulate and to provide support along the way. If they're not, they and everyone around them are in for a whole lot of hurt.

Yes, management can be an underappreciated and thankless job. There are tasks far more satisfying than handling complaints, delivering negative feedback, conducting layoffs, or confronting harmful workplace behavior like bullying, dishonesty, manipulation, or deceit. All while being attentive to the well-being of vulnerable and underrepresented team members, making sure not to inadvertently (or deliberately) prioritize those with the loudest voices. And all while ensuring larger margins and returns on investments.

However, avoiding these responsibilities only results in unhappy employees, declines in productivity, and the talent you most need looking elsewhere for better opportunities, not to mention lackluster company results.

When done well, management can be gratifying. Can you remember the last time one of your team members developed an innovative solution that saved the day? Or when you witnessed someone on your team in a state of flow, flourishing in areas that bring them joy? These moments are concrete evidence of the influence you wield, capable of positively affecting the lives of individuals, whether it's just one person or an entire team.

This is why I think of management as a calling rather than a destination. It is undeniably one of our most demanding yet most rewarding professional pursuits.

So What Can Managers Do About Burnout on Their Teams?

Everything. Imperfectly but with care, courage, practice, and commitment. This book will show you the what and how.

These days, all eyes are on managers to figure out how to hold teams together, and to prevent or eliminate burnout and productivity issues.

But how?

I've realized that expecting employees to "rebuild their resilience and engagement" through superficial solutions like vacations or benefits, which they often lack time to enjoy fully, is bound to be unsuccessful. Likewise, blaming them for their inability to keep up or fulfill every demand is futile. Why not choose an approach that heals and supports you and your teams by:

- Taking a hard look in the mirror (self-reflection)
- Examining the internal factors fueling team burnout (organizational reflection)
- Recognizing the external factors that take a toll on humans physically and emotionally (interpersonal reflection)
- Testing interventions that promote well-being and health sustainability, grounded not on assumptions but on the real experiences and pain points faced by your teams (actions)

And, perhaps most importantly, being willing to change how you manage your teams using your newfound insights.

Why This Book, and Why Now

My intimate understanding of the exhaustion and confusion that managers often contend with led me to write this book.

I've spent the last two decades driving transformational change in some of the world's most admired companies across industries such as media, entertainment, finance, and technology.

I've experienced burnout many times, often ignoring the warning signs until it was too late. However, with the support of my loved ones and guidance from experts in various fields, including leadership, wellness, and Eastern practices, I've managed to recover each time. My focus has always been on what energizes me: helping others discover their agency to become compassionate, confident, and courageous leaders.

When I speak to corporate audiences, I'm often asked to share practical advice on how to lead and manage people inclusively. Increasingly, I find myself speaking about how tough and unpredictable work can be and how managers hold the power to either uplift teams or add to their confusion, overwhelm, and burnout.

There's an abundance of books on management, some scholarly, some anchored in case studies, others anecdotal and thinly researched. This is not one of them; **it's a no-nonsense love letter to modern managers**. I'm going beyond survival mode, laying down the unfiltered truths about ourselves and our workplaces so every manager can tap into their best selves and reignite their inner fire.

My enduring belief is this: Managers need time, resources, and support to prioritize their own self-awareness and well-being *first*, enabling them to do the same for others (and us!).

Managers' collective attention—*and hearts and minds*—are overwhelmed with an unending stream of emergencies, ranging from employee crises; a reimagination of how, why, and where we work; and rapid technological advancements to widespread layoffs and budget freezes, all against a backdrop of uncertain social, environmental, economic, and global market outlooks.

From the top, there are mounting expectations to transform business operations and enhance productivity while dealing with budget cuts, enforcing return-to-office mandates, and scaling back diversity, equity, and inclusion initiatives.

Meanwhile, as managers, we are confronted with multiple demands from our teams—requests for flexibility, varied compensation and promotion expectations, the elimination of structural inequities, the assurance of safety and certainty in an uncertain world, autonomy and connection, and the support for caregiving, mental health, and well-being (bearing in mind that most managers even 20 years ago dealt with none of these issues, certainly not at today's magnitude or intensity). Indeed, these are the challenges of our times, and they demand nothing less than the full attention of every manager.

I have found that the most difficult and rewarding challenge of this work is to seek light amidst the darkness, discover strength from depletion, and seek alignment and ease even when the systems and people around us seem determined to break us. It's a ridiculously hard journey, but it can also be a liberating one—and the most important one you will make as a leader.

I share my leadership journey, enriched with case studies and research-backed, pragmatic solutions, navigating the whirlwind of a global pandemic, a racial reckoning, an economic crisis, and the social tensions of our times.

I invite you to open up to the possibility of enhancing your understanding of the physical and emotional cues we often overlook, both in our personal experiences and within our teams.

If you manage people, performance, productivity, and resources, this book is designed for you.

If you lead only one person or run a 100,000-person company, this book is for you.

If you constantly find yourself walking a fine line or in default mode shaping, guiding, and supporting stressed-out teams, this is the guide for you.

If you believe that empowering managers to prioritize dignity and well-being yields the greatest positive impact on teams and people, this book was written with you in mind.

And if you're worried about how to manage people well in these dizzying times where everyone is struggling with destabilizing interpersonal tensions, overwork, fear and uncertainty, and the resulting burnout, this book is what you've been seeking.

Think of this book as your "how to" manual to thrive in the rapidly evolving landscape of modern management. Together, we will explore how to understand ourselves and others through bewildering workplace complexities, unlocking the keys to becoming the manager every person deserves.

What Are You in For?

Structured into four parts, each chapter addresses the evolving dynamics of the modern workforce and encourages you to reflect on what may have served you well in the past or held you back, acknowledging potential limitations and then purposefully deconstructing those old paradigms to create space for new and expanded possibilities. It will take thought, practice, and courage to build your fire-fighting muscles.

Each chapter is a deep dive into the art and science of leading people in unprecedented times with personal stories, research-backed insights, case studies, and battle-tested strategies.

Finally, at the end of every chapter, I've provided scripts, which are my top picks for handling all situations. While I don't suggest reciting them robotically, I recommend honing your ability to craft scripts that help you convey the right information at the right time. Mastering this skill equips you to tackle everything from polished meeting presentations and easygoing chitchat to offering and receiving critical feedback. Let them help you corral your thoughts, vanquish pesky doubts, and supercharge your confidence. Moreover, scripts act as a shield, protecting you from you! With a script in hand, you're less likely to blurt out inappropriate or hurtful responses.

I invite you to read the chapters sequentially as intended or select the ones that speak most to you.

And finally, as you read this book, I encourage you to make room for your mind, body, and heart to heal.

Ready to become that leader you've always wanted to be?

Recognizing the Fires

1

Where There's Smoke, There's Fire: Recognizing the Signs of Burnout

"I never want to hear the word 'burnout' again!" shouted a C-suite executive.

We were having yet another return to office discussion in mid-2021, when we hoped the pandemic was finally over. Little did we know then that we still had many cycles ahead of us.

In my role as the global chief people officer, I was in the process of sharing internal and external employee data with the executive leadership team, highlighting the profound mental and physical strain the global pandemic inflicted on our workforce.

Additionally, we were trying to get our heads around the challenges of the Great Resignation, a phenomenon of massive employee resignations across every department and global office. These hurdles had managers struggling to fill vacancies and motivate employees, including themselves, as they barely hung by a thread.

I was frustrated and responded, "You can call it whatever you want, but that doesn't change the reality that our employees, especially our managers, are feeling unsafe, exhausted, and disconnected. Ignoring it won't solve the issue."

While that might not have been my finest hour, I wasn't wrong.

Breaking Down Burnout: Where There's Smoke There's Fire

Have you ever fought the urge to sneak out of a meeting momentarily, find a quiet corner, and unleash a silent scream into the void?

Have you ever found yourself drowning in a sea of employee complaints, desperately trying to stifle the urge to tell everyone to shut up?

Have you ever daydreamed about who you might be if you were burnout-free?

I have.

Visualize a version of yourself that radiates with inner light, peacefully sleeping or taking a leisurely walk in the park, instead of a you who struggles to recall not just breakfast but also the last time you savored a delicious homemade meal or shared a laugh with loved ones. It's an enticing vision, right?

Yet the relentless grind of work often clouds our dreams, making it challenging to spot the hidden triggers and subtle warnings of burnout, let alone fathom its deep-seated consequences.

In this chapter, you'll sharpen your awareness about what burnout really is—and what it is not.

Let's begin.

My Burnout Story

I've been burned out more times than I care to remember.

Burnout starts somewhere, and it varies from person to person. For me, it began as far back as I can remember.

My upbringing in the Dominican Republic—cared for by grandparents who had endured a brutal dictatorship, were compelled to leave their homeland to raise young children in a foreign country, and eventually returned as older parents to their first granddaughter—instilled within me a deep sense of maturity and responsibility from a very early age.

I not only imposed high expectations on myself to excel and be a "good girl"—whether at school, family gatherings, or social events—but also learned to suppress my own discomfort and prioritize others' needs over my own. This, regrettably, led to my failure to establish healthy boundaries and effective coping mechanisms to manage conflict and stress. My coping methods revolved around performance, maintaining a constant smile, and disregarding emotional and physical warning signals.

It turns out, I'm not alone.

For the past two decades, I've been at the forefront of revolutionizing people practices in some of the world's most esteemed companies. Occasionally, burnout episodes would wreck my patience and health despite my ninja-level skill in sidestepping and dismissing the unwelcomed, ill-mannered guests.

A catalyzing moment arrived in 2018 when I took an involuntary 11-month sabbatical due to an organizational restructuring. At the guidance of a friend and executive coach, I approached this career break as an opportunity to rest and heal my heart, which I had long neglected. I refer to this period of my life as "The Year of My Heart."

Initially, I was concerned about how this career break might impact my professional reputation and appeal to potential employers. I didn't know anyone who had ever taken career breaks. However, it became evident that this break was exactly what my heart needed.

I found joy, connection, and freedom. I took my family on far-off travel adventures, dedicated more of my time to nonprofit board and volunteer work, and cultivated a more expansive vision for my career. This experience eventually led me to the role of chief people officer at Vice Media at the onset of a global health pandemic.

While I had intended to carry my newfound learnings into my new work life, life had its unexpected twists in store.

During the COVID-19 crisis, my primary focus revolved around guiding global teams through what seemed like an endless health emergency. My daily routine was marked by providing emotional support to peers, teammates, and colleagues, offering a compassionate ear for their concerns. All the while, I grappled with an overwhelming array of work challenges that spanned nearly every time zone, crossed cultural and geographic boundaries, and encompassed both personal and operational domains, often without a guidebook. Balancing the standard HR function of recruitment, retention, and growth practices with emerging facilities concerns, reentry processes, and interpersonal tensions, and health and well-being crises that constantly popped up across teams kept my to-do list on a heavy rotation.

This tumultuous hamster wheel speed eventually propelled me down a path of prolonged burnout, an experience unlike any I had encountered in my career.

The causes of my burnout were clear: managing global teams in a 24/7 environment, shouldering the responsibility of guiding managers overseeing their respective teams, and supporting executive leaders overseeing the entirety of it all. My professional load was further compounded by the challenges of parenting a teenager and striving to be a good wife. However, as a Latina, it didn't stop there; I also attempted, and frequently fell short, to fulfill my roles as a daughter, granddaughter, sister, cousin, niece, and aunt, not to mention a friend.

It felt like my mind was constantly aflame, with every call, text, or email setting off my nervous system. But I just kept going, not making room for rest.

It wasn't just *my* burnout that needed addressing. I was also responsible for the collective burnout felt by teams worldwide, the complex operational puzzle that management and leadership teams had to untangle as a consequence, and the deep well of empathy we had to draw from while navigating uncharted waters.

Caught in this vicious cycle of performance, adjustment, adaptation, and change, I failed to notice my gradual decline in functioning. Externally, I continued to meet corporate expectations, sustaining a high level of performance. However, the relentless stressors silently eroded my mental faculties, making me feel like a sluggish sloth attempting to navigate life in perpetual slow motion.

The chronic stress I experienced also wreaked havoc on my physical well-being. Seemingly simple actions like getting up from my chair became painful, my weight and gut health spiraled into disarray, and I grappled with persistent rashes and inflammation that left me feeling like my body was aflame. I even found myself constantly scratching my skin, needing to hide the unsightly rashes.

As a child, I was that kid with an ever-present runny nose, sitting in front of the TV because any other activity felt too arduous. Asthma and recurrent bouts of respiratory illnesses were my constant companions. As an adult, the vivid childhood memories of struggling to breathe inspired me to lead a healthy lifestyle, engaging in physical activities, especially running, to strengthen my lungs.

However, after contracting COVID-19 in April 2021, I began experiencing familiar and debilitating respiratory symptoms, which were diagnosed as either long-term COVID-19 or chronic bronchitis, depending on which medical opinion I listened to. This time, my age and heightened stress levels contributed to further debilitation. My physical and emotional reserves were depleted thanks to the relentless barrage of professional challenges pummeling me since 2020. It felt like I had completed a grueling marathon filled with unexpected twists and turns, leaving me feeling fractured, worn, and constantly struggling to catch my breath. In my quest to find relief and breathe more easily, I consulted numerous specialists and tried various treatments.

A pulmonologist concluded that I was no longer asthmatic but highly susceptible to bronchial and respiratory infections, a vulnerability exacerbated as I neared my 50s. An acupuncturist treated the muscle pain and tightness in my chest. I also engaged in personal weight training to address the bloating and weight gain I couldn't shake.

Contemplating the possibility of perimenopause and a change in my diet to address the skin irritation, I also consulted a nutritionist. Upon testing my blood, her unequivocal diagnosis was that my hormone levels were at the lowest end of the spectrum for someone my age. Curious, I asked, "What do you think might be causing this?" Her response was swift and direct: "Sustained stress." The sobering reality of her words left me profoundly shaken.

"What in the world is sustained stress?" I wondered, diving into the rabbit hole of definitions.

Sustained stress, or chronic stress, is when your mind and body are in a never-ending tug-of-war, stretched to their limits. According to the American Psychological Association, it's the kind of tension that just won't quit, thanks to ongoing stressors like work dramas, financial troubles, relationship roller coasters, health upheavals, or even environmental shenanigans. And guess what? Chronic stress isn't just a minor inconvenience; it's the sneakily harmful troublemaker that messes with your mental and physical well-being.[1]

Adding fuel to the cauldron of my burnout, as I dedicated myself entirely to work, I unintentionally distanced myself from the people who cared about me the most, intensifying the toll that burnout exacted on my life.

I felt disoriented and perpetually fatigued, trapped in a relentless activity loop without the rest and replenishment that my body craved. I was burnt crispy and I neglected it for far too long.

Workplace burnout is real, a pressing challenge in work environments worldwide. However, it's something we can both prevent and manage effectively.

But first let me explain what burnout is—and what it isn't.

What Burnout Is Not

Bad days at work, though unwelcome, are an inevitable aspect of professional life. Commuting delays, printer malfunctions, Wi-Fi outages, annoying coworkers, and time-consuming administrative tasks can be frustrating, but they come with the territory of work. While these common workplace irritations might provoke negative emotions and grumbles, they're usually tolerable with a touch of good-natured griping and old-fashioned patience.

But they're not signs of burnout.

Even in well-managed organizations, work isn't always neatly distributed. Urgent client needs, unexpected market developments, and economic fluctuations can disrupt the balance. Crunch periods of concentrated efforts to meet specific, unforeseen objectives can be demanding. However, if they are brief, sporadic, and thoughtfully managed, they need not have a lasting negative impact.

A study by Christina Maslach and Michael P. Leiter estimated that 10% to 15% of employees exhibit signs of extreme burnout. The majority, however, fall into four other work experience categories: overextended, ineffective, disengaged, and positively engaged, with the latter being the most common at about 30%. This suggests that over half of the workforce might be treading in a precarious stress zone. While not in the critical area of burnout, they could be inching closer to it, balancing on the edge of one or two stressful workplace dimensions.[2]

My colleague's outburst mentioned earlier was partly influenced by the idea that workers toss out the term "burnout" as a weapon against the everyday workplace nuisances we all encounter. Burnout may not have the best reputation in leadership circles, but dismissing its significance is misguided, and it keeps you from building self-awareness and compassion at work.

Real workplace burnout is tightly linked to one's job and packs a more substantial punch than the routine tensions and annoyances on the job.

If you're feeling burned out by talk of burnout, you're not alone.

So What Is Burnout?

While it's tempting to think we coined the term "burnout" in the 2020s, did you know that the concept of organizational burnout originated in the 1970s? Yet it wasn't until 2019 that the World Health Organization, in its International Classification of Diseases, defined "workplace" burnout as an occupational phenomenon resulting from chronic workplace stress that has not been successfully managed and classified.[3]

Cait Donovan, the host of *Fried: The Burnout Podcast,* offers another definition of burnout: "the slow decline of normal functioning in every aspect of life that happens due to chronic stress."[4] When she first shared this definition with me, I had an immediate and visceral reaction. It left me momentarily speechless as its familiarity struck a chord deep within me. I instantly reproached myself for neglecting, fighting against, and denying the signs of burnout in nearly every role I held. Just as quickly I realized that this self-criticism was counterproductive and had contributed to my own experience of burnout.

Burnout is a tricky monster.

What Are the Signs of Burnout?

Simply put, burnout at work is characterized by persistent feelings of exhaustion, cynicism, and inefficacy resulting from overwhelming job-related stressors. That coworker known for their collaborative demeanor who recently snapped at you when you asked for a last-minute favor? That could be a sign of burnout. The moment in a meeting when you temporarily blanked on your colleague from Singapore's name until someone mentioned it? That, too, could be indicative of burnout. When your usual rest periods, including work breaks, weekends, and time off, feel more like "meh" than refreshment and replenishment. Additionally, when you struggle to differentiate between a genuine offense and someone simply misspeaking, these could be signs of burnout.[5]

Another sign of burnout? The Sunday Scaries.

As far back as I can remember, my aunt Maritza, a retired schoolteacher turned administrator, had an aversion to Sundays. It became a recurring family joke that we knew not to disturb her or invite her to family gatherings on Sundays. If you inquired about the reason, she would say, "I despise Sundays. If I'm too active on a Sunday, my Monday becomes unbearable, setting the tone for the entire week. I need to emotionally prepare myself for returning to work. I also hate Mondays."

The term "Sunday Scaries" describes the heightened stress and unease individuals experience as they anticipate the upcoming workweek. This can result in physical symptoms like headaches, anxiety, stomachaches, and depression. And it can manifest, as it did with my aunt, in social separation.

LinkedIn has been conducting surveys since 2018 to explore the well-known phenomenon called the Sunday Scaries. According to their data, there has been a rise in prework anxiety among workers, affecting 75% of respondents, particularly Millennials and Gen Z.[6]

In 2022, the Meditation app Headspace also uncovered a concerning statistic: almost 30% of its users struggle with sleepless nights on nearly four evenings a week, mainly due to the fear of job loss.

Dr. Dana Udall, the chief clinical officer of Headspace Health, explains, "Research has shown a correlation between economic uncertainty and stress, so this concept isn't necessarily new. However, what is unique in today's current environment is the compound effect of multiple global crises coming to a head at once—the global pandemic, political unrest, rising inflation, and economic instability to name a few. All of these factors can impact how we show up in the workplace—and ultimately our overall mental health."[7]

When managing the Sunday Scaries, their recommendations are grounded in self-care, such as ensuring adequate sleep, setting boundaries to shield against work-related emails and weekend distractions, practicing mindfulness and meditation, fostering gratitude, and seeking therapy. Taking breaks from the news and work when necessary are also helpful ways to reduce the Sunday Scaries.

What else could help? Getting clear on personal goals and celebrating achievements, which can lead to regaining motivation and purpose at work. And if none of that works, try planning your Monday schedules, easing into the week instead of jumping to a stressful Monday discussion with difficult coworkers, and creating opportunities for connection with coworkers who can lighten your spirits and offer support.[8,9]

While these coping mechanisms can benefit many, they often fall short of addressing the underlying causes of this overwhelming feeling. We frequently try to tackle work-related stress by urging individuals to enhance their resilience, all the while overlooking the fact that it's a systemic problem demanding a comprehensive solution. Regardless of the coping strategies employed, they cannot alleviate the Sunday Scaries stress deeply rooted in working conditions.

> Based on research by Christina Maslach and Michael P. Leiter and the World Health Organization, these are the three dimensions of workplace burnout:
>
> - Sustained feelings of exhaustion: Feelings of energy depletion or emotional exhaustion
> - Depersonalization: increased mental withdrawal from one's work and pessimistic or cynical feelings toward one's work
> - Professional inefficacy: reduced sense of efficacy, even failure, at work[10]

Why Workplace Burnout Matters

Ever heard of the Great Resignation, the Big Quit, or the Great Reshuffle that swept through the workforce in the early 2020s, with a mass exodus of employees across various industries? While the COVID-19 pandemic led to nonstop, overwhelming work demands, various long-established workplace conditions have exacerbated the difficulty in retaining talent.

Burnout isn't just significant as a psychological outcome; it's also tied to how dedicated people are to their jobs, careers, effort, relationships, and adaptability to organizational changes.

Decades of research shows an association between workplace burnout and a host of negative organizational, psychological, and even physical consequences, including:

Organizational
- Absenteeism
- Job dissatisfaction
- Presenteeism

Psychological
- Depression
- Insomnia
- Psychological distress[11]

Physical
- Heart disease
- Headaches
- Musculoskeletal pain[12]

Burnout Risk Factors

What complaints do workers have about the workplace, and are they valid? According to Maslach, Leiter, and Jackson, the main factors driving workplace stress and burnout include:

1. Unsustainable workload
2. Perceived lack of control
3. Insufficient rewards for effort
4. Lack of a supportive community
5. Lack of fairness
6. Mismatched values and skills[13]

Anyone who has ever had a job has likely encountered several of these situations, at least occasionally. These experiences often serve as amusing material for TV shows and films that depict people feeling worn out or fed up with work. Consider, for instance, the comically cringeworthy work scenarios portrayed in iconic TV shows and movies like *The Office, Mad Men, The Devil Wears Prada,* and *Office Space.*

Cait Donovan's Holistic View of Burnout Factors

Cait Donovan has crafted a comprehensive framework that extends beyond the workplace model of Maslach, Leiter, and Jackson. It's a masterfully woven web of modern, interconnected factors, painting a rich picture of what contributes to the risk of burnout. She categorizes these factors through a lens of holistic insight, breaking them down as follows:

1. **Work:** Encompasses elements such as workload, limited autonomy, absence of a supportive community, inequality and unfairness, lack of praise and recognition, a misalignment of values,[14] plus a deficiency of psychological safety within the workplace

2. **Culture (primarily in the United States):** Includes the glorification of hard work, emphasis on individualism, relentless pursuit of achievement, conformity to gender roles, the presence of various 'isms' such as racism, sexism, anti-LGBTQIA discrimination, ableism, and so on, and the impact of advertising and marketing on societal values

3. **Family:** Includes intergenerational trauma, unexamined familial value systems, cultural pressures within families, situations where children take on parental roles (parentified children), the presence or absence of psychological safety within familial relationships, attachment styles, and the presence of chronically ill family members

4. **Self:** Includes traits and behaviors such as perfectionism, the tendency to prioritize others over oneself (people-pleasing), challenges in setting and maintaining boundaries, difficulty seeking support, an overwhelming sense of personal responsibility and self-sufficiency, the absence of clearly defined personal values, and the presence of trauma

5. **Health:** Includes chronic illnesses, mental health disorders, the influence of genetics and epigenetics, traumatic brain injuries, and dietary factors

6. **Environment:** Encompasses the lack of access to green spaces, limited exposure to natural light at dawn and dusk, feelings of physical insecurity at the neighborhood or home level, the presence or absence of beauty in one's surroundings both indoors and outdoors, and the availability of a supportive community[15]

Cait Donovan's model is the ultimate "connect-the-dots" puzzle, explaining where all these complex factors intermingle and can lead to burnout. To her expanded list we can also add relationships with money, immigrant status, and countless others. It's as if life decided to play a little game of "Let's see how many ways we can stress you out!" But, in all seriousness, her well-researched insight is a powerful reminder of the need to comprehend the intricacy and breadth of factors that impact our well-being and those under our care. This understanding allows us to protect it and potentially keep burnout at arm's length.

So What About Managers?

This book is designed for managers who wear the hats of task-mastering, vision-guiding, and human-caring. To manage a top-performing team, you must steer tasks in the right direction while infusing your approach with strategic vision, expansive thinking, and a focus on human-centric care.

However, here's the twist. You won't succeed unless you're attuned to the signs of burnout, both for yourself and your crew. Achieving the right balance between your responsibilities and the well-being of your team is all part of the daily grind.

"Daisy, I want you to know that I appreciate your efforts in writing these manager notes, but honestly, they're not making much of a difference," said a mid-level manager to me one day. This conversation unfolded after I had sent out numerous manager Q&A documents aimed at helping managers prepare for the myriad questions and concerns their employees might have as we geared up to return to the office.

As the pandemic began, we recognized that managers were on the frontlines, bearing the weight of responsibility for their teams, clients, and audiences. They had an outsized burden to provide care, direction, and information during these uncertain times. In response, my team and I created "Manager FAQs" for various critical events to support them. These FAQs covered a wide array of topics, including our responses to racial crisis events, the health crisis, the future of work, media reports on our company's financial status, available resources, and our extensive measures, initiated in response to COVID-19, to ensure a safe return to the office.

These FAQs were designed to guide discussions, but as this manager pointed out, they fell short in addressing the increasing demands from their own managers and employees. She continued, "I'm burned out. I haven't been able to fill all the positions I need on my team. There's no assurance that we won't experience another round of layoffs. Plus, we're not offering sufficient incentives for people to return to the office. No set of FAQs can assist me in convincing my team to come back."

I was at a loss for answers. She was right. What she laid out were all the operational blockers that I couldn't solve for, and neither could she. No amount of scripts could help.

Managers serve as the linchpins in shaping the work environment, influencing team dynamics, and setting the tone for a balanced work-life culture. To successfully handle their responsibilities and achieve the organization's goals within their team context, managers must foster trust, loyalty, and motivation, all while boosting engagement, job satisfaction, and productivity. They need a toolkit with specialized influence, empathy, and relationship-building skills. Gone are the days of the old-school "do as I say because I said so" command and control mantra. Try instructing a Gen Zer to meet a project deadline without providing context and using an intimidating and fear-inducing tone. Good luck with that.

Managers face heightened workloads as we navigate the turbulent 2020s, marked by waves of restructuring, layoffs, and budget cuts in almost every sector. This surge is not just a byproduct of the usual challenges; it stems from adapting to ever-changing workflows, integrating new technologies, and operating with smaller teams under tight budgets. They're also steering through the twists and turns of new hybrid work models and enforcing return-to-office policies, often at odds with employee preferences.

Considering the mounting challenges inherent in this role, it's not surprising that managers often retreat into their silos, become isolated from colleagues across the organization, and experience higher rates of burnout and disengagement than their team members. When they are unable to receive and provide the necessary support, they inadvertently contribute to both their own and their team's burnout.

So, what can a manager do?

Gallup's 2023 State of the Global Workforce, an annual survey that helps determine employed adults' day-to-day emotional experiences at work, found that job unhappiness is at a staggering all-time high. Fifty-nine percent of people reported being emotionally detached at work, 44% as stressed at work, and 21% feeling anger. Only 23% reported feeling engaged—which is at an all-time low.[16]

The study's findings reveal that worker dissatisfaction isn't solely tied to the number of hours worked, work-life balance, or the workplace setting. Surprisingly, worker disengagement increases for remote and four-day week workers, while stress levels rise for those working in-person and on a five-day schedule. The nature of one's work schedule and location matter to a worker's well-being but doesn't tell the whole story—workers can experience unhappiness regardless of whether they're at home or in the office, working 30-hour or 60-hour weeks.

Gallup research further revealed that 55% of managers are exploring new roles, compared to 49% of individual contributors.[17] This leads to a question: How can organizations alleviate manager burnout, enhance their ability to lead effectively, and encourage their retention?

What matters, and has always mattered, is how individuals experience their work—particularly how they are managed, coached, and treated.

Lousy managers equal lousy work vibes.

According to Gallup, your manager or team leader is like the DJ of team engagement, responsible for a whopping 70% of the groove. In other words, how folks feel about their daily grind matters more in stress reduction than their seat location. So to combat the prevalent job grumbles, zombie-mode workdays, and burnout, we need workplace sherpas, not just comfy chairs. Gallup estimates that low engagement costs the global economy US$8.8 trillion, about 9% of global GDP.[18]

Takeaways from Gallup:

1. In most companies today, your people are just warming seats, not owning the stage. Ignoring these "meh" employees means ignoring a key driver of keeping customers and achieving growth.

2. Let's set the record straight: employee engagement isn't about turning your office into a happiness spa. You're missing the engagement boat if your metrics only measure employee contentment. Real engagement means your people are mentally dialed in. They know the score, have what they need, and have a supportive workplace community, perhaps even a best friend at work, a rockstar manager, and a mission they believe in.

3. Those silent quitters on your payroll? They're the ripest fruit on the productivity tree, ready to be plucked if you treat and coach them right. The worldwide average is about one engaged employee for every one sleepwalking colleague. But Gallup found that, among their top-ranked companies, it's a staggering 18 to one. Big or small, these workplaces feel different.

What's a Manager to Do?

Research conducted by Humu, a platform dedicated to driving organizational behavioral change, has uncovered a troubling statistic: one in three employees experiences anxiety while at work. Just think about it—a third of your workforce is grappling with stress![19] It's no wonder that, as revealed in Gallup's 2023 report, 59% of employees are quietly disengaging, a phenomenon referred to as "quiet quitting." These individuals are psychologically detached from their employers, exerting minimal effort, and are more likely to experience stress and burnout as they grapple with feelings of disconnection and disappointment from their workplace.

Research indicates that when we understand the root causes of burnout in our workplaces, whether they relate to specific workplace challenges or the nature of work itself, we can identify systemic solutions that can help mitigate or avoid these symptoms for workers and organizations.

Let's delve into work-related burnout conditions one by one and explore potential solutions, deepening our understanding of ourselves and the strategies we can employ to alleviate or extinguish them.

Excessive Workload and Expectations

Problem: This one's the universal troublemaker wreaking havoc on everyone. A key contributor to burnout is the relentless pressure to cope with overwhelming workloads and impractical expectations, often compounded by reluctance or apprehension to explore alternative methods to meet these demands.

Ever had that sinking feeling when someone innocently asks, "What's your work schedule like today?" The mental math alone can make your stomach churn. While our inner voices may be urging us to stop and take a break, our performance-driven instincts push us to keep going at full throttle. It's a symptom of our ingrained culture of overwork, where long hours, juggling multiple roles (including the often invisible work or "the job within the job"), and the relentless pursuit of unattainable goals have become the new normal.[20]

Try This:
- **Explain the "Why" and "What":** Transparency requires a level of courage and generosity that we sometimes fail to offer. Fostering genuine connections within teams is essential in a dynamic, fast-paced

setting where priorities are constantly evolving. When making decisions that shift a team's goals, share the rationale behind those decisions and reassign tasks as needed. Encourage team members to ask clarifying questions to ensure everyone understands roles and responsibilities, and core requirements.[21]

- **Offer Meaningful Growth Opportunities:** Don't just pay lip service to psychological safety; genuinely listen and believe your people. Work hard at creating an environment where every employee feels at ease when asking for assistance or proposing the elimination of unnecessary tasks to alleviate their workloads. Foster a culture that encourages employees to brainstorm potential solutions. Provide support for their experimentation to determine which ideas are most effective. Nurture their personal and professional development, steering clear of expecting them to wear a "superhero cape." Above all, guarantee that speaking up will not lead to negative repercussions, shame, or disconnection.

Lack of Control and Autonomy

Problem: Not having a voice or control in work matters directly impacting you can take a toll on your well-being. Unfortunately, traditional workplaces have often restricted worker autonomy. Employees subject to micromanagement or constrained decision-making authority are at a heightened risk of burnout. Despite research highlighting micromanagement, restricted decision-making, and a lack of control as substantial predictors of burnout, managers who distrust their employees or impede their ability to make valuable contributions persist in extinguishing their employees' aspirations and enthusiasm.[22]

Try This:

- **Guide Without Overwhelming:** When your team members run into roadblocks, think twice before swooping in to save the day, even if it might seem tempting. While well-intentioned guidance is undoubtedly important, an excess of suggestions on how to perform a task can come across as micromanagement, complete with the eye-rolling reaction. Instead, consider posing open-ended questions, such as "What are you trying to solve for?" "How would you propose tackling this challenge?" or "What potential follow-up questions do you foresee from the client or your colleagues?" This approach empowers team members to contribute their lived experience perspectives, granting them the agency we all desire. It also helps avoid execution errors, as they are frequently the ones closest to the solutions.

- **Spread Leadership:** Now, please don't give me a side eye here. The objective is to empower team members to assume leadership roles and responsibilities at various organizational levels. Think back to your career's early days and how being entrusted with a special assignment boosted your confidence and sense of competence. Encourage team members to share their perspectives on which tasks to tackle and how to execute them efficiently. Delegate authority and place trust in your team to make decisions, recognizing that their choices may diverge from your own without necessarily being incorrect. When mistakes occur, provide support and guide them toward solutions rather than imposing soul-crushing directives. Spreading leadership across your team is like chicken soup for the soul.

Inadequate Work-Life Balance

Problem: Thanks to technology, the line that used to separate work and personal life has become about as clear as a smudged whiteboard. The constant connectivity through smartphones and the rise of remote work has made it impossible for folks to switch off from their jobs. Sure, technology makes everything easier and more accessible, but with that accessibility comes the pesky sidekick of 24/7 direct contact and demands that erase the once-distinct borders between your time and everyone else's. A study published in the *Journal of Applied Psychology* gave us the data to back this up, showing that those struggling with maintaining a work-life balance are more likely to find themselves singing the burnout blues.[23]

Try This:
- **Flexible Work Arrangements:** Encouraging flexible work schedules or well-balanced remote work alternatives hands the reins back to employees when managing their time. Numerous studies have

shown that flexible work arrangements are a game-changer. They bring the magic trifecta of improved work-life balance, professional growth, and job satisfaction.

These benefits extend beyond employees and positively impact managers and organizations as well. When flexible work options are available, encouraged, and well-balanced among team, managers find it easier to engage, recruit, retain, and enhance productivity.

Moreover, it's a win-win for the employees in flexible work situations, who can better prioritize their tasks based on their peak focus and energy hours. The result? A boost to efficiency and job performance.[24]

- **Set Boundaries:** Setting and maintaining clear boundaries not only liberates you from frustrations and miscommunications but also contributes to a healthier, more joyful, and respectful work environment.

    Your team or colleagues may look to you for stability, courage, and wisdom, but it's essential to remember that your time, energy, and attention are finite resources. You can take simple steps like turning off work-related notifications outside of working hours or consider instituting policies that discourage after-hours emails and meetings for nonessential work matters. Remember that you set the tone for these boundaries, and openly sharing your needs and preferences makes it more likely for others to follow suit.

In her article "How to Set Healthy Boundaries When Starting a New Job," Melody Wilding advises taking into account various aspects of your work-life balance, including:

- The start and end times of your workday
- Response times for emails and messages
- Calendar blocks for focused work or "no meeting" time
- The frequency and duration of breaks during the day
- Resource or training requirements necessary for your job
- The type of work that aligns with your preferences and bandwidth[25]

In "A Guide to Setting Better Boundaries," Joe Sanok suggests committing to boundaries for at least one quarter and assessing your experience with both qualitative and quantitative measures.

You can use the following questions to track your progress:

- What positive outcomes have resulted from the boundaries I've set?
- Have there been any negative consequences associated with these boundaries?
- How do I feel now compared to how I felt at the outset of implementing these boundaries?
- What adjustments or changes are necessary to stay on course and address any negative outcomes?
- Which boundaries are non-negotiable (hard boundaries), and which are more flexible and aspirational (soft boundaries)?[26]

Low Levels of Management and Leadership Support

Problem: The core of poor management often stems from fear, and it can be exacerbated by inadequate support, communication, recognition, and a lack of respect, all of which can worsen burnout.

A management study by Humu found that 95% of employees believe that bad managers worsen workplace issues. Furthermore, following the pandemic, managers appear to be declining in their ability to listen, provide feedback, and communicate transparently—critical elements for employees to perform their roles effectively and with clear guideposts.[27]

The associated organizational costs of poor leadership and management are substantial. Gallup's research on workplace burnout reveals that employees facing burnout are 2.6 times more likely to seek a different job actively, with burned-out employees being 63% more likely to take sick days.[28]

Simply put, bad managers mess with everyone's experience.

Try This:
- **Train Your Managers Well:** Sustainable change emerges through the gradual (read: long-term) integration and reinforcement of behavioral shifts. When developing management training programs,

the objective should be to cultivate competent, compassionate, and courageous leaders, with training aiming for the following outcomes. Managers who:

- Provide support by listening and identifying tensions and stressors, including their own, engaging in open and courageous conversations, and providing resources to help employees effectively manage their workloads

- Engage in direct and empathetic conversations, enabling them to understand employees' needs and address concerns

- Employ conflict resolution techniques to swiftly address issues early on, preventing them from escalating

- Utilize stress management techniques to navigate stress and guide employees, particularly during high workload periods or crises

- Ensure equitable and sustainable workload distribution among their teams

- Challenge their own assumptions and fears while also fostering an environment where their team members feel safe to do the same

- **Meet Them Where They're At:** How often do your direct reports need to talk to you? Are more frequent, informal one-on-one meetings beneficial for certain members of your team? As a manager, understanding what your team members require based on what they're navigating at work and in their personal lives allows you to enhances your decision-making skills and enables you to offer more effective and tailored coaching support.

Each person has unique preferences, strengths, and needs, and may stumble at varying points throughout their career. Ask how you can best support them to achieve their best performance and well-being. For example, if someone prefers biweekly meetings but is currently dealing with a demanding project, onboarding several new team members, and managing elderly care, you might suggest meeting more frequently for quick checkups until things stabilize a bit.

Workplace Culture

Problem: Workplace culture is frequently the unspoken but pervasive force in the room. We may avoid discussing it openly because it can be uncomfortable, but its influence permeates every interaction and decision. Negative workplace cultures have a strong connection to burnout and various psychological health issues. Whether you are actively contributing to this culture, experiencing its harmful effects, or both, its impact is unmistakable. It's not surprising that work environments characterized by interpersonal conflicts, bullying, discrimination, or harassment provide fertile ground for burnout.

Try This:

- **Champion a Drama-Free Culture:** These days, it may not always seem so, but managers hold the reins when it comes to workplace dynamics. Communicate thoughtfully and fully own your team's results without pointing fingers at others or external factors—it all rests on your shoulders. Consistently apply rules with fairness. When making a decision, consider the impact it will have on every individual and own your decision. Instead of assigning blame, dive into self-reflection and ask, "What might I be overlooking as a cause for this disruption?" or "How can I help connect the dots better across and between teams?"
- **Stop Being Complacent:** It's hard because we're often afraid of calling out what's messing with our cultures. But someone has to do it and that someone should be the person guiding the team. Steer clear of passive-aggressive behaviors like making excuses, showing favoritism, orchestrating secretive campaigns, or playing the blame game. Instead, cultivate trust and break down silos through open dialogue, meaningful connections, and relationships that provide you with the insights necessary to make fair and well-informed decisions.

Insufficient Rest and Recovery

Problem: Adequate rest and recovery are often overlooked, leading to an increased risk of burnout. In her book *Rest Is Resistance*, Tricia Hersey highlights the pervasive issue of "grind culture," prioritizing constant work and productivity at the expense of rest. This work culture often leads us to neglect reparative practices like unplugging from social media, slowing down or engaging in activities that help us reconnect with our minds and bodies.[29] Ignoring our body's and mind's signals makes us susceptible to chronic stress and burnout and can harm our overall health. A 2022 report from the World Health Organization underscores the importance of health as an investment within the broader societal context. It emphasizes the pivotal role of rest in promoting overall health and well-being.

Try This:

- **Lead by Example:** Setting the tone starts at the top, and you are the one you've been waiting for. Look no further. Encourage, guide, and inspire yourself and the managers on your teams to uphold boundaries, safeguard their physical and mental well-being, and champion the importance of rest.

- **Plan for the Unforeseen:** Support employees in allocating time for unexpected moments by encouraging them to include buffer time in their schedules. Respect these designated periods and avoid encroaching on them like an inconsiderate chat message. Furthermore, promote a flexible approach to task management that enables employees to adjust to unexpected challenges as they arise.

Women and People of Color: What's Seen and Unseen

Women and people of color often face compounded workplace stressors due to additional expectations—some self-imposed and others imposed by societal pressures. These expectations include providing emotional support for the organizational culture and taking on various unseen responsibilities that consume their time and resources. Unfortunately, these contributions frequently go unpaid, unrecognized, and unrewarded.

To truly break free from the burden of unfair labor practices and the ease with which our society and workplaces benefit from this hidden work, we must begin by exposing it to the light.

In her *Time Inc.* article "How to Put an End to the Inequities of Unseen Work," S. Mitra Kalick highlights the disproportionate impact of invisible labor on women and individuals from marginalized communities.[30] She draws attention to the insights of Leah Goodridge, the managing attorney for housing policy at Mobilization for Justice. Goodridge points out that women often invest significant time and effort in nurturing and sustaining relationships with colleagues, clients, and stakeholders—a practice that is essential for business success, teamwork, and productivity.

Furthermore, Goodridge sheds light on the tendency for people of color to assume a "supporting character role," as she aptly terms it. In this role, individuals of color find themselves frequently called upon by their white colleagues to provide emotional support and help identify, analyze, and offer insights into systemic issues within their respective institutions. This dynamic places an additional, often unacknowledged, burden on people of color, further illustrating the pervasive impact of invisible labor in our society.

Let me make it very clear: Black people, women, marginalized people, really no one, owes you their emotional labor. And it's burning them from the inside out.

When you add the factors that disproportionately prevent women, people of color, and other marginalized communities from advancing in the workplace, including microaggressions, double standards, the experience of being "an only," and bias, among others, it becomes evident that their exhaustion levels have risen to unmanageable levels.

Workday blunders may not be necessarily fueled by racist, sexist, or oppressive intentions. Nevertheless, when such experiences have been a part of your personal history, it can be difficult to interpret them in any other manner. This can contribute to additional dimensions of burnout.

It can feel overwhelming, unmanageable, and simply impossible, but in the modern workplace, every manager's responsibility includes identifying the signs of burnout. Consider the impact you can make by being attentive to what might be negatively affecting your team members and building new management muscles through strategies aimed at enhancing their well-being. Ready to learn more?

Let the Sparks Fly: How We Grow

Now that we've explored the signs and impact of burnout, what it is, and its nuanced expressions of depletion, I invite you to reflect on the following questions as you embark on the journey to reclaim your inner spark as a manager:

- Who would I be if I was not burnt crispy?
- What is preventing me from becoming the best version of myself as a healthy leader?

Remember:

- Burnout is not a scoreboard of your shortcomings.
- When your employee tells you they're burned out, listen and uncover sources of exhaustion or discontent.

- What works: manageable workloads, a sense of purpose, fairness, trust, connection, and psychological safety.
- What you can do: Highlight the "why," offer meaningful growth opportunities, guide without overwhelming, spread leadership, design flexible work arrangements, set boundaries, train managers well, meet employees where they're at, champion a drama-free culture, banish complacency with poor behaviors, and lead by example.

Scripts for Managers:
These scripts are tools for managing workplace stress and burnout for yourself and your team. They encourage open dialogue, self-care, and a focus on growth, critical elements in maintaining a healthy work environment.

When you're feeling the heat rise and depletion begin, consider reciting these mantras:

- I choose calm.
- I am safe.
- I trust in my ability to lead my team.
- It's OK to pause, rest, and replenish.

When an employee approaches you about their burnout or you sense that their reactions may be signs of burnout, consider asking:

- What comes up for you emotionally or physically when you come to work or join a meeting?
- What do you think is driving your feelings about your work environment?
- How, if at all, have your feelings toward colleagues and work changed in the past 6–12 months?
- How can I help?

PART

II

Navigating the Flames

2

Show Up: How to Manage Multiple Fires

On a Friday evening during the COVID-19 pandemic, I received a call that shook me.

A senior executive, his voice trembling, informed me that his teenage daughter had attempted suicide. He was desperately trying to connect with our benefits providers after hours, seeking immediate help for her as she lay in the hospital, in need of stabilization at a residential mental health treatment center. He feared that the place she would be sent to might not provide the care and support she urgently required.

My heart sank.

Although it wasn't explicitly in my job description, this wasn't my first encounter with an employee-related suicide attempt. However, this hit me on a personal level.

Through getting to know each other, we discovered our daughters were of the same age and exchanged heartfelt stories about our families. His daughters were the center of his world.

"I'm so sorry you're going through this. You are not alone. We are here to support you." I assured him. I immediately assigned our head of benefits to oversee his case personally and also asked our most senior HR business partner to reach out to him for additional care and support.

As I detailed the resources available to him and assured him of my availability throughout the weekend, he responded with a heavy heart, "Thanks so much. My head is spinning. This is unbelievably hard. My heart is broken. Again, apologies for reaching out over the weekend."

After I had conveyed all the necessary information through email, texts, and phone calls, I put my hands down and allowed myself to cry.

Once I had collected myself, I went straight to my daughter's room. She was engrossed in TikTok videos, and I held her close. My husband and I frequently talked with her about her feelings, friendships, and schoolwork, reinforcing that we were her safe haven. Nonetheless, like many parents of teenagers, we couldn't always be entirely certain about what was going on in our kid's mind and heart.

But what I did know is that holding onto the pain from life's infernos and also creating a space for those enduring such pain was slowly consuming me from within.

The Fires of Managers' Lives

How can you tell if you're on the fast track to burnout or already extra crispy? A good indicator is to reflect on how frequently you run around with a metaphorical fire blanket, dousing flames left and right.

One of the senior managers on my team once said to me, "Daisy, I've got three fires to take out. Which one do you want me to get to first?" Sadly, this situation is all too familiar—a recurring "cleanup on aisle one." We're trapped in a relentless cycle of crises, struggling to recover from one before the next hits. Our days are consumed by firefighting, and our teams are on the brink of burnout from all angles.

Here's news that's a surprise to no one: workplace stress thrives on overwork and interpersonal tensions. Throw operational blunders and social, market, environmental, and economic turbulence into the mix, you've got a recipe for a burntout team and managers feeling extra crispy. These are the daily fires that managers must extinguish, often multiple times a day. But it's not just about putting out the fires; we also need to be there for our teams, modeling care and resilience to guide everyone through to the other side.

Whether in corporate boardrooms or professions like teaching and nursing, everyone's grappling with historically high levels of burnout.

Even tried-and-true practices aren't cutting it anymore. I once received advice from a mentor, suggesting that around 20% of my time should be allocated for unforeseen events and unexpected situations. However, today's complex and unpredictable global landscape demands significantly more time and emotional resources, from handling rising political tensions and racism to reimagining work, economic challenges, xenophobia, environmental crises, and beyond. How can we show up for our teams and ourselves under these circumstances?

Reflecting on the challenges my team and I faced during the pandemic, maneuvering through organizational dynamics and craftily utilizing corporate resources only took us part of the way. We also needed to lend a listening ear and a compassionate heart as our colleagues navigated their darkest hours, which seemed to stretch into eternity. Our emotional skills were constantly put to the test, and our reserves were depleted daily.

We were all dragging ourselves through a broken system with less support, fewer structural solutions, and limited breathing space, trying to fix it one piece at a time. While I tried to protect my team's emotional well-being, mine was ablaze. I couldn't possibly show up for every fire they had to manage or the difficulties they faced when I was barely hanging on. I knew something had to change, and it required deep self-reflection, guided by my leadership coach, to find clarity on how I wanted to lead while honoring my well-being.

In this chapter, we will explore how to show up in five of the common fires managers face nearly every day: employee crises, operational blunders, geopolitical risks and market uncertainties, interpersonal tensions, and the messy returns to the office. I will share ways to create a supportive team environment, make thoughtful decisions, and navigate these issues without succumbing to burnout.

With each fire, I'll show you how reigniting your light amid the volatile and uncertain fires we face at work can be challenging, rewarding, and possible.

Let's start with what consumes much of our time: employee crises.

Employee Crises

▌ "Do you ever feel like you're failing at everything as a manager?"

I frequently notice uneasy expressions and awkward laughter when I ask this question during my conversations with managers and leaders. My goal is to help them rise above the fog of self-doubt and reassure them that it's normal to fail in our jobs occasionally. We all experience bad days at work, unsuccessful projects, disheartened teams, or dissatisfied clients. Moreover, effectively handling both the operational and human aspects of their job is their duty and entirely achievable. My approach in these talks mirrors how I support my team—combining tough love with empathy. I get the toll managing an employee crisis can take on one's body, mind, and spirit— the importance of getting it right—for our well-being and the benefit of those we lead and collaborate with.

When your company includes employees scattered across various geographies and time zones, something bad is bound to unfold for someone at any given hour of the day. These challenges can range from family and friend deaths, which unfortunately increased during the COVID-19 era, to previously undiagnosed ADHD or bipolar conditions, children facing rare diseases, cancer diagnoses, divorce, eviction, and, as I mentioned earlier, far too many instances where suicide was contemplated—just to name a few.

No matter how adept one becomes at navigating distressing moments in others' lives, it's impossible to avoid the emotional toll. We all require support, resources, and a compassionate listener to put one foot in front of the other. This helps prevent our internal fires from escalating due to either regret over unsolved problems or the profound impact of these issues when they hit close to home.

On March 27, 2022, I wrote a message to my team addressing the commonly known "Sunday Scaries." I had noticed that team members were expressing anxiety about upcoming workweeks, and I decided to confront this issue directly. I began by sharing my coping strategy for dealing with these feelings, which involved crafting weekly notes to them. These notes served a dual purpose: they allowed me to reflect on the past week and prepare for the upcoming one, all while maintaining a meaningful connection with folks across different geographical locations. The subject line for that Monday's note was "Withstanding Change and Challenges."

In the message, I acknowledged that we were facing an unusually high rate of resignations across the company and within our team, primarily due to a hyper-competitive job market and employees experiencing exhaustion and disconnection. I owned my role in ensuring that our team felt valued and motivated to stay. Our employees were not OK, and we were not OK. My intention was to offer tools that could help them regain their equilibrium.

To wrap up the message, I shared this quote from Oprah Winfrey's book *What I Know for Sure*:

Every challenge we take on has the power to knock us to our knees. But what's even more disconcerting than the jolt itself is our fear that we won't withstand it. When we feel the ground beneath us shifting, we panic. We forget everything we know and allow fear to freeze us. Just the thought of what could happen is enough to throw us off balance. What I know for sure is that the only way to endure the quake is to adjust your stance. You can't avoid the daily tremors. They come with being alive. But I believe these experiences are gifts that force us to step to the right or left in search of a new center of gravity. Don't fight them. Let them help you adjust your footing.[1]

In what I hoped would serve as a soothing message, I underscored that the challenges we had faced managing turbulent situations for employees worldwide had contributed to our growth as professionals, colleagues, and friends. I urged them to view supporting employee crises as part of our mission rather than something to resist. I encouraged them to find their footing in these challenges and to ask for help whenever they felt unsteady.

As managers, our daily mission is regaining our balance and wading into situations with care and clarity—not just for ourselves but for each other and the people we support. I believe this approach can work for any team, including the employees you're guiding or supporting, and it's like a secret sauce for their personal growth and well-being.

Operational Crises

Work-related operational predicaments can take on various forms, whether it's dealing with CEOs making premature announcements about restructurings and workforce reductions, managing situations where leaders or brand-sponsored talent make offensive public comments, addressing controversies like offensive imagery in college dorms, or navigating regulatory concerns like those faced by General Motors' Cruise self-driving cars regarding public safety regulations, resulting in motions to halt production.[2] These crises can also include diversity and inclusion scandals, extreme weather conditions, or data leaks.

When these crises hit, organizations often shift into all-hands-on-deck crisis management mode, allocating significant time and resources to mitigate their impact on brand reputation, operations, and overall performance. These challenges can persist for weeks or even months, prompting everyone to retreat to their respective bunkers and disrupting the well-being and burnout protection measures of all those involved.

The toll on managers during an operational crisis is undeniable. Questions like "What just happened? Can we hit the pause button, please?" and "Would anyone be kind enough to give us a breather?" echo in their thoughts. These high-pressure situations demand rapid thinking, resource reallocation, and decision-making in the face of extreme uncertainty. Managers frequently find themselves working marathon hours, sacrificing personal time, and carrying the burden of immense stress to steer their teams through the crisis. The weight of responsibility for the organization's performance, reputation, and the well-being of employees can feel as heavy as an elephant on their shoulders, leading to burnout, anxiety, and exhaustion that can rival the endurance required for a marathon. Moreover, the emotional toll of making difficult decisions, such as layoffs or restructuring, can persist long after the crisis has subsided, much like a stubborn tune you can't get out of your head.

And then there's the daily grind that never takes a coffee break. For a manager, operational responsibilities include:

1. Driving results
2. Continuously assessing your team's readiness to adapt and thrive in the face of future challenges while attempting to close skill gaps
3. Efficiently managing workloads and resources to ensure optimal performance
4. Cultivating a culture of collaboration and innovation to drive ongoing improvement

I've frequently felt like the reigning champion of letting my team down. Picture this: after months of excitedly announcing and meticulously preparing for the launch of a new and improved performance management system, we had to break the news to our employees that they'd have to return to the old-school method of inputting their performance reviews on dusty Google documents. Why? The company had stopped making payments to the vendor due to funding pressures.

Helping my team bounce back from the disappointment was a responsibility I would have gladly traded for just about anything else. They had poured their hearts and souls into this project, fueled by my high expectations and their genuine enthusiasm. But then we had to hit the reset button, and the weight of knowing our jobs just got a whole lot tougher felt like a lead balloon.

I concentrated on what I consider a fundamental requirement for all organizations—wholeheartedly prioritizing the mental and emotional well-being of my team, particularly those who had their workloads double due to the process disruption. I pushed back deadlines, expressed my regret about our circumstances with a hopeful outlook for better days, carried the heat by communicating with the company, and made every effort to offer whatever support they needed to minimize the lasting impact of this latest ordeal. Nonetheless, I wondered: Was it enough?

From my viewpoint, maybe not, but I showed up for them when it mattered. Although they were aware that the situation was far from ideal, when everyone needed a helping hand, they valued knowing that—at the very least—I had their backs.

Geopolitical Risks and Market Uncertainties

Is it just me, or does it feel like I'm the only one who remembers that bad things were happening all over the world before the COVID-19 pandemic turned our lives upside down? The past four years have been so tumultuous that it's easy to forget that life has always had its ups and downs. Or is it harder to recover now because the ebbs and flows are so close together?

I can't help but think back to that fateful morning after the 2016 US elections when I was living in California and working at Google. I had to break the news to my then 10-year-old daughter, whose innocent question about the election results still haunts me. She looked at me with concern, started crying, and said, "But he doesn't like people like us," pointing to her brown skin. Those days were painful, confusing, and worrisome. And so are our current times.

Fast forward to the COVID-19 pandemic, the most recent meta crisis etched in our memories. Alongside it, we've witnessed the rise of hatred campaigns against Asian communities born out of unfounded fear, a surge in anti-Smitism, anti-Muslim sentiments, the Hamas-Israel war, the war in Ukraine, economic recessions, the ascent of right-wing movements, and countless tragic deaths.

We know that social and economic conditions beyond the workplace can exacerbate feelings of burnout within the workplace. In a world marked by relentless turbulence, uncertainty, and disruption that permeate every facet of our lives, it's no wonder that workplace burnout rates continue to climb. The strains from geopolitical and market tensions only add to the weight that managers bear in these tumultuous times.

> You make people feel anything is possible. it's really effective—it's probably why I took this job. Paul does the same thing—that anything is possible. But it isn't real, Cory. It's all smoke and mirrors, and I thought that was the difference between you two, but now, I'm not so sure.[3]

In this quote from *The Morning Show*, Stella, a prominent network executive, fearlessly challenges Cory, the network's CEO. She acknowledges Cory's talent for projecting an image of boundless possibilities but questions its authenticity, likening it to "smoke and mirrors." When she declares that her trust in him has been shattered, it resonates with numerous conversations I've had with employees who have questioned the motives and sincerity of their managers and organizational leaders, including me.

Over the course of my career, I've learned this: leaders and managers have to ethically balance truth-telling with hope, resilience, and optimism. If managers don't maintain a sense of possibility and inspiration, even when facing challenges and uncertainties, they risk their teams losing their faith and giving up. It's a cascading effect that can't be understated.

Navigating layoffs is an emotionally charged journey, and as managers, we've had our fair share of navigating this bumpy terrain, especially in challenging macro-environments. Yet it's even tougher for employees, those directly affected and those who stay.

In these moments, lean on the basics of leading people: take responsibility for the decisions (even if you didn't make them, your team look to you for clarity), acknowledge the missteps that may have led to the need for a layoff (don't hide behind the higher-ups or economic trends if that's not that truth), treat outgoing employees with the respect and dignity they deserve, show empathy for the challenges and feelings people may have, create multiple avenues for folks to check in, ask questions, and express their emotions, keep communication channels open for ongoing updates, be visible and accessible, and reassure remaining employees about the company's mission and commitment to their well-being and the continued success of the business.

Now, I get it; after conducting layoffs, you might feel like you've just run a marathon while juggling flaming torches. The conversations, coordination, last-minute hiccups, and emotional responses can be draining. But here's what I've learned: managing through the human impact of these decisions with care is not only the right thing to do, but it also enhances the well-being of your team. It can shield against burnout, even during challenging times.

Five Tips for Modern Management

I'm often asked for advice on managing people, particularly regarding handling tensions in today's modern work environment. Here are some insights I've gained about managing the most critical needs of our teams—their agency, inspiration, and wellness:

1. **Tackle the Elephants in the Room:** Engage candidly with your team about workload, expectations, and concerns to build trust, sprinkle zen, and boost morale. Talk it out, even if it's scary, weird, or uncomfortable, and create room for others to do the same.

2. **Recharge Your Batteries and Theirs:** Turbulent times require abundant energy and resilience. Don't just give wellness a nod; give it a bear hug. Prioritize downtime for your team, encouraging breaks and disconnecting from work. Don't forget Employee Assistance Programs and vacation days. Reserve time for self-care on your calendar, set boundaries, and respect the boundaries of your team members.

(continued)

(*continued*)

3. **Acknowledge the Feels:** Many of us are still sifting through the unhealed impact of chaos; care and empathy are necessary. Seek understanding of the emotional impact of turbulence on your teams and acknowledge diverse needs and communication styles. Recognize and appreciate your team's efforts and accomplishments. Hold off on the judgment and scrutiny; empathize and feel their feels first.

4. **Ask Better Questions:** Leadership is an ongoing commitment that gets a turbo-boost in a crisis. Continuously seek feedback from your team to identify areas for improvement and growth. What inspires them, what gets in the way at work, what can be done better, and what don't you see?

5. **Take Flexibility Seriously:** Set and keep realistic goals and deadlines to reduce the overwhelm. Offer formal and informal flexibility, including remote options or flexible hours. Pro tip: If organizational priorities or market conditions shift, be flexible too. Give your team agency over their work-life balance by moving less critical goals, pushing back deadlines, and keeping your team's sanity intact.

A Word About Crisis Management

Ever wanted to just say, "Make the news stop!"?

Throughout the pandemic, I was repeatedly reminded that leading people under the weight of crisis demands a unique skill set, including a deep reservoir of strength, courage, and resilience, distinct from executing standard operational tasks. We all have limitations when dealing with change, and it's not always about the individual but their capacity to endure change, whether in substantial doses or relentless waves. I often told my team I tried to wear my leadership and management badge with confidence, compassion, and care, but I didn't always get it right. There were times when I wasn't patient, kind, or generous with colleagues, the individuals we supported, my team members, and even my boss.

Institutions across the United States, from corporations to college campuses, have experienced heightened emotions and tensions sparked by a range of issues, from heartbreaking losses to enduring turmoil, including protests and counterprotests about wars, racial and religious conflict.

Figuring out how to talk respectfully, fairly, and factually about charged issues can be tricky, whether at the family dinner table or in virtual workspaces. This became particularly apparent following the tragic death of George Floyd on May 25, 2020, and was again further felt in the wake of the Hamas terrorist attack on Israel on October 7, 2023.

Having witnessed the profound effects of these events in workspaces, universities, and communities, this is what I typically advise managers grappling with the daunting task of deciding how and when to navigate conversations about local or global crises:

1. Start by seeking as much information and resources as possible, including gaining a comprehensive grasp of the situation, its ramifications, the organization's role and position, and the available resources.
2. Consider language that resonates with your team. I've used "respectful arguments" over what has become the somewhat watered-down term "courageous conversations."
3. Establish clear boundaries for your role and your team—understanding what it entails and, perhaps more crucially, what it does not—and make sure they are honored.
4. Exercise caution when taking sides in contentious matters, share balanced and reliable news insights, and avoid making premature predictions about possible outcomes.
5. While the desire to solve every issue is understandable, it becomes daunting when faced with various sources of pressure. As managers, we must remember this principle for ourselves first: "Put your oxygen mask on before assisting others."

The most effective approach I've found is demonstrating care for your team, reinforcing company values and policies related to maintaining respect and communicating your responsibilities and limitations to employees. Unrealistic expectations can be like that persistent fly you can't seem to swat away, reminding you of their presence every other hour or so.

Sometimes, in a world of madness, showing up for others means showing up for yourself first.

Interpersonal Tensions

What's the most common workplace fire, you ask? It's the everyday human tensions that inevitably arise in daily interactions. Managing these tensions can feel like dealing with an unruly bonfire—emotionally draining not only for yourself but also your team and colleagues.

I've witnessed the detrimental impact of unaddressed interpersonal tensions and toxic behavior on organizations. Subtle racial slights, nasty attitudes over a sense of entitlement, disagreements over project deliverables, and gossip about perceived unfair advantages can significantly disrupt team performance, collaboration, and productivity. They create operational friction within teams, leading to disengagement, mistrust, and demotivation among employees. And they take a toll on culture, health, and well-being.

I frequently remind my teams, "I can't solve problems I don't know about," and "Please bring me the whispers before they become screams." However, trust is essential for employees to confide in you and disclose the truth. Without trust, team dysfunction festers.

I once faced the task of addressing a situation marked by intense anxiety and dysfunction between two teams. A senior leader, unhappy with the support from a shared service model, loudly insisted on replacing an employee outside his direct reporting line. This demand upset everyone involved—the targeted employee, their managers, and the leader making the accusation. From the outset, here's what I understood:

1. There was no evidence that the senior leader had given constructive feedback to the targeted employee or their managers before the eruption.
2. This leader had a history of demoralizing peers and junior colleagues through unreasonable expectations and micromanagement.
3. Collaboration across these functions was essential to deliver a successful product.

To efficiently resolve the matter, we brought everyone involved together for an open discussion aimed at identifying the root cause of the tension that was hindering teamwork. At first, junior team members were hesitant to voice their concerns, so I stepped in to facilitate the conversation, ensuring an environment of fairness and transparency. We candidly addressed service quality, engagement guidelines, and communication processes while preserving everyone's dignity and respect.

Within fifteen minutes of the cross-functional meeting, we identified the sources of operational friction:

- An excess of decision-makers
- A lack of a shared operating agreement
- Style preference misalignment among decision-makers

Had we dismissed the senior leader's comments as "just how he is" or avoided a mediated discussion due to fear of retaliation, we would have allowed the situation to escalate further, potentially resulting in emotional outbursts or the resignation of valuable team members.

I can't claim that we resolved every tension within that team or that the manager in question fully rose to the occasion, recognizing his mistakes not only in his management style but also in how he treated a junior team member and the example he set for others. However, we prioritized protecting the dignity of the junior employee, modeled restorative justice conversations to restore relationships, and shared the burden with those experiencing pain on the ground. We try, we show up, and we continue to make efforts to improve.

In a *Harvard Business Review* article, "How to Proactively Defuse Tension on Your Team," I offer five steps to root out interpersonal tensions and toxic behaviors, many of which may lead to burnout.[4]

Even minor incidents such as subtle racial slights, disagreements over project deliverables, or gossip about perceived advantages negatively affect team performance, collaboration, and overall productivity, and can lead to prolonged overwhelm and frustration. They can create team friction, leaving employees disengaged, distrustful, and unmotivated. Factors including differences in personality, perspectives,

(continued)

(*continued*)

racial, class, and gender privilege, work and communication styles, power imbalances, and a lack of transparency and clarity regarding work processes and business objectives are often the leading cause of these tensions.

Here are five steps to reduce interpersonal tensions and toxic behaviors in the workplace:

1. Identify the root causes of workplace tension, such as power imbalances and differences of opinion.
2. Seek to understand others' perspectives and nurture trust among colleagues to resolve misunderstandings.
3. Choose the right time to address issues or seek support, considering the impact of your words and actions.
4. Don't hesitate to seek help from HR or other resources in navigating difficult situations and promoting a healthy workplace.
5. To repair harm and trust, acknowledge the impact of your actions, take steps to make amends, and commit to behavioral change.

These approaches, grounded in open communication and empathy, can help handle everyday workplace tensions. However, when these solutions merely act as temporary fixes for ongoing, relentless stresses in the workplace, burnout can emerge and lead to significant exhaustion.

Messy Returns to Office

"Daisy, tell me, why should I come to the office?"

This question was raised by a manager in London during a hybrid presentation, both in-person and virtual, aimed at people managers on my least favorite topic: our return to the office. Up until then, I had tried to alleviate the rising anxiety by calling it "our ease back." I initially thought that easing people into a new context in their work lives would make the transition easier and that when they came back they would be so happy to be among their peers and colleagues that everyone would want to rush back to the office—three days a week. I couldn't have been more wrong.

I had just outlined all the safety measures we had implemented to make the office space post-pandemic safe. I passionately made the case for returning to the office, emphasizing the energy, camaraderie, and quick problem-solving that happens when we work in close proximity. And I urged them to consider how returning to the office could reinvigorate our way of working, boosting productivity, fostering connections, and enhancing collaboration—all in alignment with our mission and goals.

I tried to strike an empathetic balance between the importance of face-to-face interactions and the liberating flexibility of deciding how, when, and where we work on days not assigned to office work.

I concluded by saying, "We're built for this! And we're building what's next together." Despite also providing FAQs and tools to assist them in transitioning their teams back to the office, I got a healthy dose of side-eyeing from Singapore, London, and my own Brooklyn backyard.

The managers didn't budge. Their employees didn't budge. And the same could be said for our leadership team, who looked to me to make it happen. Sure, we brought more folks back to the office, but often grudgingly and never at the volume that leadership hoped for.

I dreaded every one of those conversations and messages. It often felt like I was trapped in a never-ending, chaotic scene from the movie *Everything Everywhere All at Once*. While it's unrealistic to believe we can resolve every issue for each individual, the expectations at every level just keep coming our way.

Navigating the return-to-office landscape is akin to facing an uncontrolled fire; nobody knows how to extinguish it. Business leaders like Elon Musk, Mark Zuckerberg, David Solomon, and Jamie Dimon have been determined to return their workforce to the office.[5] At the same time, employees increasingly crave the autonomy they gained during the pandemic.

Amazon's CEO, Andy Jassy, boldly pushed employees to return, and the fallout left managers grappling with the consequences.[6] Despite its divisive nature, there's no playbook to guide these decisions, and leaders want a return to the old ways, while employees want to retain their newfound flexibility.

Surveys consistently show that strategies for returning to the office are not working, fueling internal conflicts about productivity and company culture. Working remotely, especially for women with caregiving responsibilities and intersecting identities, offers more than just flexibility. It provides psychological safety and increased productivity.[7] However, implementing these new work arrangements falls on managers, who are caught in the crossfire between leadership and employees.

Just when I thought I'd seen it all, a new wildfire ignites—a sizzling topic that lingers and singes everyone in its path, from leaders and managers to board members.

These days, discussing flexibility and hybrid work tends to elicit discomfort, sighs, or outright concerns. The extra fire on the cauldron? While the leadership teams call the shots, managers—not the decision-makers—bear the brunt of implementing these new work arrangements.

According to the 2023 Flex+ Strategy Group Research Report, work flexibility has two levels: individual and organizational. Individual flexibility empowers employees to choose when, where, and how they work, facilitating work-life balance.[8] Organizational flexibility is about the where, how, and when of getting work done. When these levels align, organizations benefit from higher revenue, increased profitability, better talent retention, improved employee engagement, and enhanced workforce well-being.

Bringing teams back to physical workplaces may seem a routine organizational task, but it has become one of modern management's most daunting and polarizing challenges. It's like trying to tame an uncontrolled fire, and if not handled correctly, it can also burn you.

Surveys from the Conference Board to Gallup keep beating the same drum: the strategies for getting back to the office just aren't working.[9,10] The internal conflict primarily centers on two major issues. One is an ongoing debate about whether these evolving arrangements and policies benefit productivity and company culture. And two is the growing chorus of voices questioning the wisdom of demanding a return to the office today.

Senior leaders ask, "Why are folks reluctant to return to the office?" They've heard countless times that most workers don't favor a full return to the office and that caregiving responsibilities are taking a toll. But they seem to remain indifferent.

How about asking, "Are managers and leaders coming to the office?" Look around—they don't want to come in five days a week either.

It's OK to say, "Given the nature of our work, you have to be in the office (these many days)." But at the same time, managers and leaders have to adhere to the policy. When you're in the office, are you visible and setting an example for others? Are you making it worthwhile for someone to come in and collaborate with others? Or are they stuck to screens all day doing the same thing they would have if they stayed home? You gotta make it worthwhile for everyone.

Emotions are running high and working in any context is messy, but there's no avoiding the impact of these fires. It's crucial to gain clarity on what's essential, listen to your teams, take one step at a time, and guide your team through this next stage in the ongoing evolution of the workplace.

The Urgent Now

Do you ever cringe at cryptic texts or emails with subject lines like "check in" or "quick chat"? Those low-key requests can send shivers down a manager's spine, signaling either a full-blown crisis or the faintest hint that something's amiss, ready to turn into a blazing fire at any moment. Staying alert for those silent alarms waiting to pounce on our unclaimed calendar slots can burn us to a crisp.

In times of crisis, employees turn to their leaders for guidance, comfort, and a roadmap to navigate the uncertainty ahead. But what happens when their leaders and managers are also in crisis?

In moments of overwhelming chaos, clarity in decision-making is your friend. The idea that clarity and alignment magically appear as the clock ticks down is often wishful thinking. Instead, vital leadership decisions usually demand to be made right in the middle of all the chaos and commotion.

To navigate daunting choices effectively:

- Break them into manageable steps to focus your attention and unlock possibilities.
- Understand that the path to a solution involves making focused decisions, not impulsive ones.
- If you're knee-deep in chaos, don't rush; take it slow. Remember, slow is smooth, and smooth is fast.

Let's build leadership clarity by taking it one step at a time:

Step 1. Assess the Type of Decision Required

In the face of constant pressure and distractions, take a moment to consider whether maintaining focus and avoiding overreaction is the right path. Sometimes, the wisest decision is to pause.

Effective leadership must step in decisively when chaos engulfs from multiple angles and circumstances become irreparable. Avoiding action might be perceived as denial or avoidance. So, take a moment to pause, assess, and decide on the most appropriate course of action.

Step 2. Get Clear on What Needs Resolution

Managers often get stuck in the decision-making web, wrestling with questions such as "Should we make this decision?" and "How should we implement it?"

A manager's skill is anticipating what's next, identifying risks, and strategizing ahead. Yet this foresight can become an obstacle when concerns over subsequent actions slow down decision-making. Avoid indecision. Acknowledge that eliminating all risks is unfeasible, and delaying decisions only heightens uncertainty and anxiety. Once the decision is clear, act decisively.

Step 3. Put Plans into Action

After a clear decision is made, the focus shifts. Instead of dwelling on hypothetical fears and conflicting emotions about decision-making, acknowledge hurdles and choices, and involve others. Identify who needs to know in what order, set clear expectations, support those processing the decision, allocate additional resources or feedback discussions as needed, build coalitions of support across the organization, celebrate progress, and ensure those who must step up receive the necessary support. In times of significant change, everyone wants to know: "What does this mean for me?" Deliver clear responses. While not all decisions will be welcomed warmly, well-communicated and decisive choices can cut through chaos and build followership and support.

Remember, clarity is your ally in pulling your team out of the noise. People need and appreciate clarity, even in the face of tough decisions. I'm not advocating for a culture of entitlement where every complaint is indulged, but rather an environment where employees feel empowered to bring their questions, suggestions, and best selves to work. Sometimes this might mean offering reassurance through memos or direct conversations; at other times it may necessitate candid discussions.

A case in point is a senior manager who once told me their wish to admit in their performance review: "I need clarity and more time. I am increasingly burnt out and struggling to focus on the big picture because I fight fires all day and night. I must be in a position to think about the next 18–24 months because the seeds of that are sown now." Yet they hesitated to express this to their leader for fear of being misunderstood or embarrassed.

This scenario is not unique. The relentless stress caused from constant fires makes it increasingly difficult to find individuals who are ready and willing to take on management roles. The never-ending grind is burning us out.

The challenge we all face is to not shirk our responsibilities as people managers, even when we're battling unfathomable fires. My hope is that we become more skilled at leading ourselves and the people we serve, knowing when to act, pause, or stop to regain our balance. This includes learning how to rebuild trust in ourselves and others when adversity leads us astray, taking our needs and those of our teams seriously, and putting out fires with clarity rather than exacerbating them.

Let the Sparks Fly: How We Grow

Now that we've explored the delicate balance between empathetic leadership and personal well-being when facing multiple work fires at overwhelming speeds and workloads, it's time to listen to your own voice. Reflect on the following questions and scripts to help you regain your grounding and reignite your inner spark as a manager:

- How has your perspective on global events and market uncertainties evolved in recent years, and how has this impacted your personal and professional life?
- Have you encountered or observed workplace burnout within your team or organization? What were the contributing factors, and how did they affect productivity and well-being?
- In your role as a manager, how do you balance candid truth-telling and nurturing hope and optimism, especially during challenging circumstances?

Scripts for Managers and Teams

Managers:

1. "Remember, you're not navigating this alone. We are a team, and I'm here to offer my support. Please share your concerns and needs."
2. "I take full responsibility for the operational blunder. Let's discuss solutions to rectify the situation and prevent it from happening again."
3. "I have confidence in your judgment and would appreciate your insights on how we can adjust and thrive as a team in these uncertain times."
4. "I'm here to support you. What specific steps or support would be most helpful for you in navigating this moment smoothly?"

Teams:

1. "I appreciate your support during this latest crisis. It means a lot to know you're here."
2. "Thank you for acknowledging the operational mishap and working toward a solution. Your transparency is valued."
3. "I've been researching market trends and geopolitical risks that might affect our projects. I'd love to discuss my findings with you."
4. "I have some concerns about safety and flexibility. Can we talk about how we can address these issues as a team?"

By promoting open, empathetic, and collaborative communication, managers and their teams can navigate unforeseen challenges while maintaining dignity, well-being, and a healthy, productive work atmosphere.

3

The Hulk with Heart: Holding People (and Yourself) Through Your Rage

"I rage-wrote that plan," a senior manager on my team confessed as I thanked her for rapidly devising a path forward to handle another unforeseen workforce management crisis in the company's sales process.

At eight months pregnant, she was the only HR leader on my team with the technical expertise to manage the necessary tasks. She carried a load on her shoulders, mentally and emotionally, that extended beyond the already physically demanding creation of a new life. The burden of guilt for placing such asks on her weighed heavily on me.

We had been alerted to a time-critical issue on a Sunday afternoon. By Monday mid-morning, she delivered a detailed project plan, including task assignments, risk assessment, budget, dependencies, change management considerations and contingency plans. Her precision in every detail aimed to maximize our scarce resources.

While we chuckled at her remark about "rage-writing" the plan, I couldn't help but be concerned about the toll this intensity was taking on her.

In this chapter, I share what it looks like to hold the people you lead and yourself through the inevitable rage that arises in the high-pressure stakes of modern workplaces, and how to handle the emotional demands of leading people without losing clarity, composure, and compassion.

Look Out!: Why Managers Lose It

Remember Bruce Banner transforming into the Hulk when he got angry? That sudden shift from mild-mannered scientist to a towering, green, rage-filled monster? That's what it's like when we lose our cool! We go from mild-mannered managers to angry, green monsters.

In my experience with organizational crises, I've seen myself and my team regularly become Hulk-like figures, driven by the intense emotional stress of daily challenges. Yet instead of granting physical power, these frequent shifts into our alternate egos overwhelmed our capacity to be present in our work and drained our spirits, edging us closer to burnout.

As a people manager, I was the designated emotions and concerns holder. My team, those backstage heroes, safeguarded our culture and people operations, often feeling neglected, underappreciated, alienated, and mistreated by those they supported. It was all part of the gig, but it's challenging not to let those circumstances wear you down. While we might have shared Hulk's less desirable traits, we lacked any actual superpowers to fall back on.

Picture a shattered old-fashioned thermometer, not the sleek modern one. Similar to how mercury scatters uncontrollably when these thermometers break, my frustration, along with that of my team and colleagues, spilled into all areas of my life. Trying to rein it in was no small feat—my patience frayed, my empathy wore thin, and even straightforward solutions seemed to slip through my fingers. My reserves of social, mental, and physical energy took a nosedive, and anger became my default response. Before I realized these were burnout symptoms, I just kept pushing through.

Righteousness: The Hidden Danger

When audiences ask me how to handle disagreements about workplace diversity, equity, and inclusion efforts, I emphasize the importance of not letting righteousness become a barrier. Righteousness acts like a wall, preventing people from seeking shared understanding and co-creating solutions. It can trigger your inner Hulk in a matter of moments.

Of course, that's easier said than done.

Humans are inherently judgmental creatures. We often misinterpret conversations, hold ourselves and others to unfair expectations, and create narratives that can lead to tension and disharmony in our personal and professional relationships.

At work, this tendency can disrupt efforts to align managers, leaders, and employees. Managers might perceive their employees as fragile and overly sensitive, adopting a superior and dismissive stance, while employees may experience their superiors as detached and ineffective, breeding resentment and mistrust.

We spend far more time trying to be understood than trying to understand ourselves in relation to others, a tendency I've observed in various work relationships, from colleagues to managers.

Looking back on my professional life, from enjoyable experiences with cooperative colleagues to struggles with unsupportive managers and difficult team members, I've noticed moments when I lost patience too quickly or reacted harshly when I've been in pain. I've had my own "oh no" moments, unintentionally disappointing others. Facing this truth, I followed the advice I often give managers: I turned the mirror on myself and asked, "What role have I played in letting others down?" and "How might my actions or inactions contributed to mistrust or tension in working relationships?"

Confronting these questions wasn't easy, but it was necessary. It's a journey every manager should embark on, pushing past discomfort to build understanding, empathy, and open communication. Why? Being in constant conflict with those around us leads us to a burdensome sense of unease that undermines our leadership abilities and well-being.

In management, righteousness often acts as a hidden danger, subtly yet significantly eroding team dynamics. I've witnessed managers, deeply entrenched in their viewpoints, inadvertently overlook the valuable insights of their team members. For instance, a manager in a media company, convinced of a traditional marketing approach, ignored a junior team member's concerns regarding language in a campaign targeting Black communities. This decision not only stifled the team's creative thinking but also led to a noticeable drop in morale and a sense of alienation among the staff. It also led to painful and expensive social media backlash.

Such scenarios illustrate the far-reaching consequences of righteous attitudes, undermining both a team's internal harmony and the organization's broader effectiveness. When managers close themselves off from the frontline insights of their team, especially those most proximate to the heartbeat of the solutions they seek, they risk not only the team's spirit but also the very future of their business.

Breaking down the walls of righteousness requires basic yet powerful tools: empathy, open communication, and an appreciation for diverse viewpoints. We can replace the toxic brew of silence and mistrust with the nourishing soil of understanding and cooperation.

Affirmations to Avoid Self-Righteousness

Psychologist Dr. Audrey Tang shares a powerful technique called "Just Like Me" to shift our focus toward understanding others. This affirmation method goes like this:

JUST LIKE ME—people can have a hard time.
JUST LIKE ME—others might let you down, even when they don't want to.

She further designed a "move on" exercise to help you do just that instead of dwelling in judgment:

1. **Ask, don't assume:** If upset, calmly ask why something happened and discuss potential solutions for the future.
2. **Recognize if you are making "sweeping statements" and call yourself out on them:** Catch yourself making generalizations (like "All men/women/children. . .") and reconsider if they truly reflect your thoughts.
3. **Choose to recognize (and verbalize) something nice instead of the critique:** Replace negative thoughts with positive

observations, like appreciating someone's happiness instead of seeing it as showing off.

4. **Don't take it personally:** Consider this perspective shift: The
person who let you down is probably more engulfed in their own
life's hurdles than actively seeking to offend you.

This approach helps to diffuse anger and foster understanding,
reminding us that we are all human and "perhaps not so bad—
after all."[1]

Managing Diverse Teams in Hulk Mode

I've had my fair share of adventures in assembling and leading diverse and
intersectional teams, with each team member carrying their unique lived
experiences and, at times, traumas from their past. The pandemic led to
times when we all felt like we were transforming into versions of the Hulk,
not because we were bad people but because we were lugging around our
baggage of crises compounded by past experiences based on race, gender,
and myriad other identities and personal histories.

A lesson I've learned is that creating safe spaces and encouraging others
to share their experiences is not enough. People need to feel genuinely
heard and, importantly, believed. Offering empathy to those facing difficult
situations, with words like "Thank you for sharing with me. I'm sorry for all
you're going through," can significantly alleviate their burdens. It also
provides reassurance that their feelings are being met with understanding
rather than doubt or ridicule.

Going beyond this, sending out tailored messages to individual teams
and broader company-wide communications during times of social upheaval
can be highly welcomed. Recognizing the fears and uncertainties felt by
various communities, including those within our workplace, is necessary in
modern management. By offering relevant resources and guidance, these
communications transcend the role of performative gestures. They evolve
into vital management tools that assist in adeptly managing through complex
and demanding moments.

Here are some nuggets of wisdom from my adventures in managing teams to avoid Hulk mode:

- Listen to your employees. You hired them for their talent and ideas, so consider and implement them!
- Get comfy with the fact that you won't please everyone. Making decisions is like choosing a Netflix show with your partner—someone will grumble, maybe even walk out of the room to watch something else, but that's the trade-off of your choice.
- Empathy—don't just say it. Walk with it, merengue with it. Words are great, but actions? They're magic and pixie dust that turns our dreams from "someday'" into "right now."
- Hold yourself and others accountable. It's not a game of "who can dodge the responsibility." Clear and frequent engagement and communication are your beacon of light.
- And for the grand finale: Don't be a power hog. Share the love, spread the power. It's not a crown to be kept in a glass case; it's more like a beach ball at a concert. Toss it around!

Navigating the Tricky Terrain of Emotions That Can Trigger Your Inner Hulk

What advice would you give someone overwhelmed by constant messages of "thriving at work" when they're struggling to make it through the day?" This question came from an anonymous post during a panel discussion about leadership in the modern workplace. It deeply saddened me, and I regret not having the opportunity to sit down with this person to understand their day-to-day struggles better.

This scenario reflects the current state of many workplace interactions between managers and employees. With high emotional stakes, there's a risk of falling into harmful practices like toxic positivity or unintentionally gaslighting team members.

Toxic positivity is an overzealous cheerfulness that ends up invalidating real struggles. It's like saying "just smile!" to someone having a rough day. Not helpful. On the other hand, gaslighting is when you mess with someone's sense of reality. You know, downplaying their feelings or making them think they're overreacting. Both are more common than you'd think and can throw off the balance in workplace relationships that keeps your Hulk mode in check.

Successfully steering clear of these pitfalls requires understanding your team members. You can't demonstrate a baseline of empathy and kindness if you don't know what they're experiencing.

Reducing the burdens of your team members means genuinely listening to their concerns and avoiding responses that downplay their feelings, such as offering overly optimistic reassurances like "Everything is going to be OK." Also, keep in mind that it's not about you. Bringing your own experiences into the spotlight might unintentionally eclipse or belittle the emotions and circumstances of those you're attempting to support. Focus entirely on them—their needs and desires.

Trauma-Informed Management Lessons

Trauma at work is not new. But talking about it sure is.

Katharine Manning's article "We Need Trauma-Informed Workplaces," in the *Harvard Business Review*, draws attention to a sobering statistic: "Six in 10 men and five in 10 women experience at least one trauma." This equates to 50–60% of individuals in today's workplaces. Furthermore, approximately 6% of the population will grapple with post-traumatic stress disorder (PTSD), and up to 8% may contend with complex PTSD, often arising from prolonged exposure to child abuse, domestic violence, war, or frequent community violence.[2]

What does implementing a trauma-informed management approach involve? It's primarily about actively listening to validate lived experiences and understanding that not all environments are safe. It means reducing triggers in our language, policies, and practices and empowering team members to have a significant say in decision-making processes.

Manning shares the Centers for Disease Control and Prevention's six guiding principles for a trauma-informed approach:

1. Ensuring safety
2. Fostering trustworthiness and transparency

(continued)

(*continued*)

3. Promoting peer support
4. Encouraging collaboration and mutuality
5. Emphasizing empowerment, voice, and choice
6. Addressing cultural, historical, and gender-related concerns

She further distills them into three overarching concepts:

- Acknowledge ("I will be heard.")
- Support ("I can get the help I need.")
- Trust ("I will be treated fairly.")

For managers, these are the assurances your team members need to hear from you:

- I hear you, and, more significantly, I believe in you.
- I will do my best to get you the support you need.
- I see you as a person vital to our team and organization.

Consumed by the Job

During a catch-up meeting after her departure from the company, a former team leader shared a striking revelation with me. As she looked back on her tenure, she voiced a bitter reflection with a hint of sadness: "The greatest irony was that my role was to ensure the well-being of our employees, yet I was blind to my burnout through the never-ending crises and restructurings. I didn't see it coming. I was so consumed in the day-to-day that the crazy felt normal, and I stopped giving a damn. Only now do I realize it."

Her words made me wonder: Why do we so often push ourselves to the brink in our health and careers, allowing these relentless moments to fuel our inner Hulk? We usually only realize the need to rebalance our work and life when we're dangerously close to a breakdown or after stepping off the treadmill, sometimes to the point where we can't even recognize ourselves.

And what becomes of us when this constant state of being consumed ultimately leads to deep-seated fatigue? Even the most caring of us check out.

Work demands that engulf every aspect of life can lead to compassion fatigue. This is commonly observed in sectors like healthcare, education, human resources, and social work, where there's continual exposure to the distress of others. The pandemic revealed that these symptoms extend beyond these fields, as the previously mentioned example highlights. The unyielding nature of the modern workplace, coupled with growing emotional labor needs, often drains us, posing significant challenges for managers and employees as they strive to fulfill their responsibilities without compromising their well-being.

In "That Numbness You're Feeling? There's a Word for It," Adam Grant introduces "empathic distress," a concept relevant to management as it reinterprets traditional compassion fatigue.[3] Neuroscientists Olga Klimecki and Tania Singer identified empathic distress—initially observed in healthcare—as the inability to alleviate pain, rather than the act of caring, that leads to distress and potentially depression. This disturbance arises not from a lack of concern but from being overwhelmed by others' suffering and feeling powerless to help.

For managers, practicing compassion that understands and acknowledges harm and distress, rather than just trying to fix it, can prevent burnout. Managers need to tune into the silent struggles faced by their team members, particularly those who are disengaged. Demonstrating compassion and encouraging self-compassion within the team can transform disengagement into meaningful connections. Small gestures of understanding and kindness can significantly boost team morale and strengthen a manager's ability to make a positive difference.

On the other hand, compassion fatigue and empathic distress manifest through symptoms like chronic stress, potentially culminating in burnout. Recognizing these signs is essential for restoring balance, enhancing creativity and productivity, and achieving overall wellness.

Symptoms of compassion fatigue and empathic distress can differ and might not all occur simultaneously, but generally include the following kinds of symptoms:[4]

1. **Emotional:** Feelings of detachment, hopelessness, emotional numbing, general anxiety, frustration, cynicism, anger, and irritability
2. **Mental:** Experiences of disorientation, confusion, diminished empathy, a sense of powerlessness against others' distress, and a constant fixation on the suffering of others

3. **Physical:** Manifestations like shortness of breath, frequent headaches, heart palpitations, difficulty sleeping, and muscle tension
4. **Professional:** Episodes of overwhelm, work-related exhaustion, challenges in maintaining focus, disconnection from others' emotions, and a struggle to exhibit compassion

Help your teams find compassion for themselves and others by recognizing the pain they bear and extending compassion toward them. Remember to apply this approach to yourself as well.

Self-Compassion Quiz

This brief quiz, based on a more extensive test by Kristin Neff, associate professor at the University of Texas at Austin, can help you assess your level of self-compassion. Answer these true/false questions to gauge where you might need to focus on developing self-compassion:

1. **Self-Judgment:** I'm disapproving and judgmental about my own flaws and inadequacies. (True/False)
2. **Fixation on Negatives:** When I'm feeling down, I tend to obsess and fixate on everything that's wrong (True/False)
3. **Self-Criticism in Tough Times:** When times are really difficult, I tend to be tough on myself. (True/False)
4. **Impatience with Self:** I'm intolerant and impatient toward the aspects of my personality I don't like. (True/False)
5. **Negative Self-Reflection:** When I see aspects of myself that I don't like, I get down on myself. (True/False)
6. **Overwhelmed by Upset:** When something upsets me, I get carried away with my feelings. (True/False)
7. **Lack of Self-Kindness:** I can be a bit cold-hearted toward myself when I'm experiencing suffering. (True/False)
8. **Intolerance of Flaws:** I'm intolerant of my own flaws and inadequacies. (True/False)
9. **Exaggerating Painful Experiences:** When something painful happens, I tend to blow the incident out of proportion. (True/False)
10. **Feeling Isolated in Failure:** When I fail at something that's important to me, I tend to feel alone in my failure. (True/False)

Answering "True" to these questions suggests areas where self-compassion can be strengthened.[5]

Consider taking the full test at Kristin Neff's Self-Compassion Test https://self-compassion.org/self-compassion-test/ for a more comprehensive assessment.[6]

Mitigating Compassion Fatigue, Empathic Distress, and Burnout

Here are several strategies for both organizations and individuals, compiled from my research on various mental health platforms, aimed at mitigating compassion fatigue, empathic distress, and burnout:

Disconnect

1. **Regular Breaks, Not Breakdowns:** Make it a habit to step back from the emotional roller coaster of work now and then. A stroll, some zen breathing, or a chill moment between meetings should do the trick.
2. **Vacation, Like Now:** Nudge your team to cash in those PTO days. It's not just a perk; it's a recharge ritual!
3. **Vacay All the Way:** Protect work-free vacations. Emails can wait; mental peace cannot.
4. **Draw the Line:** Keep work and personal life in their corners. Sanity and health? Yeah, they thank you in advance.

Self-Care

1. **Healthy Habits, Happy Life:** Get enough sleep, eat well, and hydrate. Your body will high-five you back.
2. **Mindfulness:** Walk it off, meditate, or breathe deep like a yoga guru.

Commuter Options

1. **Decompression Express:** For the commuters, turn that journey into your personal zen zone. Train tracks or traffic jams, it's your time to unwind from work stress.
2. **Homebound Roadies:** Working remotely? Fake a commute. Walk, cycle, or jog around the block. Switch from home-you to work-you and back with style.

Institutional Support

1. **Resources:** Ensure that managers and teams have sufficient resources to meet work deliverables effectively.
2. **Goals and Roles:** Ensure organizational objectives are clearly communicated and directly connected to individual job responsibilities. No more mystery missions.
3. **Support Squad:** Consider bringing in employee assistance and mental health platforms like Spring Health, Lyra Health, Calm, Headspace, and others. And call in professional coaches for additional support and development. It's like having a personal trainer, but for your career.

Implementing these practices can work wonders for crafting a healthier work environment, lowering the chances of work consumption, and giving well-being the green light to thrive.[7,8]

Working Through Grief and Anger: Common Triggers for Your Inner Hulk

"Los niños hablan cuando los pollos mean." Kids speak when the chickens pee.

Hearing this phrase often during my childhood was a clear signal that our voices were unwelcome in the realm of adults. I've always loved connecting with people—it's my happiness hack! So it should come as no surprise that I was a talkative child.

One particularly vivid memory dates back to when I was around nine, visiting elderly family members. Often the youngest in these gatherings, I generally found these visits uncomfortable.

I'll never forget the afternoon that vividly etched the experience of absorbing someone's anger into my memory. I made the cardinal mistake of interrupting my grandmother with questions while the adults were engaged in conversation. I remember the deep pain of my grandmother's nails digging into my hand as we walked home. The journey felt as long as crossing a baseball stadium, though it was only a few streets.

My grandmother muttered something about how I had embarrassed her, emphasizing that she had explicitly told me *not to say anything*. Interrupting adult conversations must have offended the adults who had no patience for a candid child. They had no interest in hearing from me, and because I was an extension of my grandmother, my misstep was perceived as her failing.

Hence, her frustration. Her rage was transferred to my small body, heart, and spirit. I held back tears and apologized profusely.

All I wanted was to be heard. Instead, I was scolded and left with a nasty scar on my hand and a heavy heart. I managed to restrain my inner Hulk, but I made a solemn promise to myself: I would keep my mouth shut around adults and bury my emotions to make myself smaller. The "keeping quiet" part was not easy, but I became skilled at "shutting down," always at the cost of my agency and well-being.

That was then, and this is now. The young girl who once felt overshadowed in those tense family gatherings has since transformed, much like a reverse Hulk into Bruce Banner, and risen to work at the highest levels of the private sector. Throughout my career, I have focused on elevating the voices of others, learning to tap into my inner strength to ensure my needs and the needs of those around me are adequately met.

In the social media shame story I shared in the book's introduction, my fury resembled that of the Hulk—directed at everyone involved. It was a reaction born from feeling misunderstood, a familiar sensation that often led me to shrink to get by.

This time, I allowed myself the space to fully experience this fury, shedding tears, raising my voice, and venting my frustrations within the sanctuary of my home. I was acutely aware of the importance of not causing harm to others when I hurt, but the release of my emotions was necessary. Throughout these emotional transformations, my husband provided unwavering support and patience, gently guiding me back to a state of calmness. When it came to my interactions with my teams and coworkers, I had to summon inner strength to maintain composure.

I mourned my vision for a harmonious workplace, and a combination of crises, poor leadership decisions, ongoing tensions, and the continuous onslaught of unprecedented challenges fueled my anger.

No one wants the hassle of managing in these complex times.

Managing people has become an increasingly demanding, underappreciated, and often thankless job. Many managers who have worked hard at climbing the leadership ladder are discovering that the reality of leadership in these complex times differs vastly from their initial aspirations. Dreams of a corner office, unwavering entitlement, and a sense of authority have given way to relentless pressures, overwhelming workloads, and insubordinate teams.

To be fair, managers shouldn't bear the unrealistic burden of being superheroes nor the unhealthy results of Hulk transformations. While managers are responsible for holding teams together, overseeing intricate interpersonal, political, and legal challenges, and addressing tough issues like sudden downsizing, layoffs, leadership changes, and even bankruptcy, this responsibility should not come at the expense of their health and well-being.

Burying the Pain to Get the Job Done

"We need to change that title," our head of communications suggested when reviewing a draft article summarizing the Wrap's Power Women Summit panel discussion: "Power Women Driving Cultural and Social Change." In this panel, I, along with other women leaders from the entertainment industry, discussed the expected cultural and social challenges in our workplaces for 2023.

The original title that was proposed to us resembled something along the lines of "Vice Media's Chief People Officer Says More Impossible Decisions Will Be Made In 2023." My colleague expressed concerns that "impossible" might be misinterpreted as implying further workforce reductions. Given our recent experiences, including a painful round of layoffs and a complex sales process that ultimately didn't materialize, we couldn't risk any more harm to our company's reputation.

The National Center for PTSD defines racial trauma as "the emotional impact of stress related to racism, racial discrimination, and race-related stressors, such as being affected by stereotypes, hurtful comments, or barriers to advancement." This trauma can profoundly impact both physical and mental health, potentially leading to PTSD in some cases.[9]

This concept resonates with my personal experiences. Throughout my career, I've frequently felt muted, and even well-meaning advice has occasionally seemed like another effort to suppress my voice, blurring the lines between helpful guidance and silencing. As a woman of color, facing these obstacles has been a constant in my professional journey, intensifying my frustration. Although this particular instance may not have been an intentional act of silencing, it felt like it, contributing to the ongoing accumulation of trauma I've experienced—a bit like gradually unleashing the Hulk within, one frustration at a time.

Silence, and being silenced, hurts us.

Managing teams with integrity, competence, and courage can be a formidable endeavor, particularly when one's voice is silenced.

Suppressing our emotional turmoil to meet our job obligations is a common experience among many managers. I would contend that this phenomenon can be especially amplified for women of color, who frequently have to navigate gendered racism while striving to excel in their roles. While there may be occasions when maintaining silence is essential and even requested without any ill intent, your sensitivity to whether or not it's justified becomes heightened when you've carried the burden of being silenced.

I stood by the quotes attributed to me in the article, as they accurately represented the challenges confronted by every chief people officer and diversity and inclusion officer at that time. We were all tasked with making impossible decisions concerning people, budgets, health, and processes, all while lacking a roadmap and under constant and unrelenting pressures. Failing to acknowledge these hardships felt like deception.

However, recognizing it was the company's best course of action, I reluctantly complied.

As it turns out, I am among many women who bear substantial personal and professional self-silencing burdens, pushing ourselves to depletion.

In a *Time* article titled "Self-Silencing Is Making Women Sick," the author, Maytal Eyal, a psychologist, writer, speaker, and host of the podcast *Heal With It,* shares this advice she gives her patients: "Be more disappointing." She argues that societal pressure for women to be agreeable, selfless, and suppress their emotions is killing them.[10]

Eyal references the research of Harvard-trained psychologist Dana Jack from the late 1980s, which unveiled a consistent pattern among female patients suffering from depression: a propensity for "self-silencing." Jack's definition of self-silencing includes behaviors such as excessive caretaking, people-pleasing, and the inhibition of self-expression, all undertaken to nurture intimacy and fulfill relational needs. This behavior is intricately tied to gender norms and has been found to elevate the risk of depression.

Eyal further highlights that women's self-silencing, influenced by cultural expectations, significantly raises their susceptibility to various physical and mental health issues. Women are disproportionately affected by autoimmune diseases, chronic pain, depression, anxiety, and even premature death. She points out that women make up nearly 80% of autoimmune disease cases, face increased risks of chronic pain, insomnia, fibromyalgia, irritable bowel syndrome, migraines, and are twice as likely as men to die after a heart attack. Additionally, women experience depression, anxiety, PTSD, and anorexia at much higher rates than men, with self-silencing playing a role in these disparities. Research also connects self-silencing to cardiovascular problems, irritable bowel syndrome, HIV, chronic fatigue syndrome, and cancer.

Yes, we make ourselves more prone to cancer when we overwork!

Eyal recommends that instead of suppressing your anger or frustration, consider asking yourself, "What do I need right now?" Similarly, she promotes the idea of setting and communicating healthy boundaries as a way to foster positive relationships. The author recognizes that "such a shift requires change on both the individual and societal level, and will by no means be easy. But it's certainly worth it—after all, women's lives depend on it."

Lower the Temperature

"I am a calm leader who can delve deep into complicated matters, bridge the gap between multiple audiences, and use influence to engage others in the process," an executive-level candidate applying for a role where she would be responsible for hundreds of people once told me.

I couldn't help but give her a sly smile, thinking, "This place will rob her of this calm."

So I asked, "How do you ensure the well-being of yourself and your teams when these complex matters have a way of draining everyone's calm?" She gave me a canned response about the value of wellness and caring for her teams. I couldn't ding her for the response; it's an incredibly challenging task, especially when you don't fully know the terrain you're walking into.

Many of us need soothing, or at least a respite from the ongoing uncertainty and fear that pervade our daily lives. The relentless need for inventive approaches to safeguard our teams' well-being, deepen connections, cultivate organizational culture, and facilitate meaningful dialogue in virtual settings has drained us.

When I contemplate the idea of soothing, I remember how I comforted my daughter when she was a toddler. I would cradle her gently, matching my breath to hers to model self-soothing, Being a thumb-sucker myself until I was nine, I understood the comfort it brought her. In contrast, my husband would observe us with affection and curiosity, never having experienced the soothing sensation of sucking his thumb. (By the way, I'm not implying that you should walk around your workplace sucking your thumb.)

Currently, deep breathing is my go-to strategy. Over the years, I've experimented with various breathing practices, but my impatience typically gets the best of me. Everything changed, though, when I discovered the concept of the physiological sigh.

Getting 200 people to synchronize their actions isn't an easy feat. However, that's exactly what Megan Duelks, Physical Well-Being Lead at Johnson & Johnson, accomplished during a "Wellness Break" at Seramount's "WorkBeyond" Summit. (Seramount is a strategic professional services and research firm.)

Megan reminded the group about a similar exercise she had led the previous year, where she encouraged everyone to ask themselves three questions:[11]

1. **Am I breathing?** Hopefully, the answer is yes. But now that you're paying attention, how are you breathing? Is it shallow and rapid, indicating stress? What can you do to calm down?
2. **Am I moving?** If you've been stationary, consider taking a short walk. If you're like me, your Fitbit may remind you to move because you've been sedentary for too long. Pay attention to its advice.
3. **Am I grateful?** The power of gratitude to reframe situations is remarkable. It puts us in a better state to acknowledge and reciprocate positivity.

Megan aimed to enhance our practice on this warm fall day in New York City as we gathered in a large conference space. She emphasized the importance of breath and introduced us to the concept of the physiological sigh as the fastest way to release stressful responses in our bodies.

Everybody sighs, right? But what if we were to use it to harness well-being?

A physiological sigh is an involuntary deep breath consisting of a deeper inhalation and a prolonged exhalation. This reflexive breath, occurring periodically and often unconsciously throughout the day, resets the respiratory system and supports healthy lung function. It plays a key role in preventing lung collapse and maintaining optimal oxygen and carbon dioxide levels in the blood. Intentionally performing this double exhale reinflates small lung sacs, enhancing gas exchange, which efficiently expels carbon dioxide, promoting quicker relaxation.[12]

These sighs distinguish themselves from regular, shallow breaths involving deeper, extended inhalation and exhalation. Studies have demonstrated that even a single intentional physiological sigh can induce a state of calmness and relaxation, making it a valuable tool for managing stress and enhancing overall well-being.

Here's how it works:

1. Take one long inhale through the nose.
2. Follow it with one sharp inhale, expanding the lungs.
3. Slowly exhale through the mouth.

Every day, without fail, I take a physiological sigh that invariably transforms a rigid frown into a smile. This sigh is more than just an expression of frustration; it's a conscious act of taking something in, a moment of nourishment rather than body language complaints.

- My daughter brushes off my attempt at a hug. I sigh, and the tension dissipates, eventually.
- I'm running late, and upon arriving at my subway stop, I'm met with the dreaded announcement of "train delays, we appreciate your patience, garble, garble." I sigh, accepting that I'll get there when I get there.
- A team member reaches out to me, informing that a senior leader has mistreated yet another junior team member and asking for my assistance. I sigh, my mind clears, preparing me to tackle the issue at hand.

The beauty of this practice is that you can do it in the presence of others, and they won't even notice. It appears as a thoughtful pause, which it truly is. By harnessing this accessible tool, I immediately find myself in a better state, benefiting myself and those around me.

Sometimes we need less reaction and more breathing.

Cyclic Sighing, Who Knew?

In 2023, Stanford University professor David Spiegel spearheaded a study to compare the effects of mindfulness meditation, cyclic sighing, box breathing, and cyclic ventilation.[13] The findings indicated that while all practices effectively reduced anxiety and enhanced mood, breathing techniques outperformed mindfulness meditation in mood improvement and lowering respiratory rate. Notably, cyclic sighing emerged as the most effective, significantly boosting calmness and reducing respiratory rate more than the other methods.[14]

Spiegel attributes the success of cyclic sighing to its focus on a conscious, prolonged exhale, which likely slows down the respiratory rate and may decrease the heart rate through parasympathetic activation.

Here's how to practice cyclic sighing:

1. Find a comfortable position, either seated or lying down.
2. Begin by slowly inhaling through your nose, fully expanding your belly, then pause briefly.
3. Continue inhaling, this time expanding your chest to fill your lungs.
4. Exhale slowly through your mouth or nose.
5. Repeat this cycle for five minutes.

Considering that meditation and breathwork have been shown to improve mood and foster calmness, it's worth exploring these practices to see what resonates with you. Spiegel underscores the importance of dedicating time regularly for self-awareness and self-regulation.

He notes that investing just a few minutes daily to manage your mind and body can significantly enhance overall well-being.

"You must never confuse faith that you will prevail in the end—which you can never afford to lose—with the discipline to confront the most brutal facts of your current reality, whatever they may be."

—*Stockdale Paradox by Jim Collins*

In his book *Good to Great*, Jim Collins popularized the Stockdale Paradox,[15] drawing insights on resilience and leadership from Admiral James Stockdale's experiences as a prisoner of war in Vietnam. The Stockdale Paradox highlights the crucial balance between maintaining an unwavering faith in a positive outcome and having the discipline to confront the harsh realities of present circumstances. This principle is a vital tool for contemporary leaders facing today's unprecedented challenges.

As managers navigate the complexities of leading remote workforces and managing diverse, multigenerational teams, they often find themselves simultaneously playing the roles of boss, coach, and nurturer. Compounding their complex stewardship, managers often encounter skepticism from younger employees who ask, "What exactly do you bring to the table?" When they think they've mastered it all, the constantly evolving digital landscape presents new challenges, making it feel like they're trying to navigate a maze blindfolded. This transition from historical lessons to modern-day management dilemmas teaches us the importance of holding onto faith in a positive outcome while realistically appraising and addressing workplace challenges.

But wait, there's more! Managers are under constant pressure to achieve ambitious goals while navigating job insecurity in a market that's about as stable as a Jenga tower. One misstep can jeopardize their reputation and the company's bottom line. This precarious situation begs the question: what triggers might unleash your inner Hulk mode? Identifying these triggers speaks to modern managers' emotional and psychological strain.

These multifaceted challenges underscore the indispensability of resilience and adaptability in a manager's toolkit. And let's not forget the undeniable truth—doing it all without self-care or mental health is simply impossible. So here's to recognizing the need for a breather and acknowledging that even managers need some downtime in this wild world of work!

Sometimes We Just Need to Laugh at Ourselves

In their book *Humor, Seriously: Why Humor Is a Secret Weapon in Business and Life (And How Anyone Can Harness It. Even You.)*, Jennifer Aaker and Naomi Bagdonas, the driving force behind Stanford's esteemed business school course "Humor: Serious Business," deliver a comprehensive playbook for incorporating humor into the corporate world.[16]

Their central argument is straightforward: humor is a powerful tool, particularly for those in leadership roles. It serves as a foundation for trust and an engine for creativity. Research findings consistently affirm that when humor is part of the workplace dynamic, work teams communicate more effectively and achieve higher performance levels. In addition, employees tend to regard leaders with a sense of humor more favorably, and the feeling is often reciprocated.

However, Aaker and Bagdonas keenly observe a noticeable scarcity of humor in most professional settings. This shortage primarily stems from a fear of lacking comedic talent and the concern about unintentionally causing offense.

However, their key insight is refreshingly simple: humor is a skill that can be acquired, and its benefits extend beyond the laughter generated by a perfectly timed joke. In the context of research around job interviews, they write, "It's whether you have the gumption to tell *any* joke (which signals confidence), and whether that joke is appropriate for the context, that signals status and confidence."

Work collaborations don't always have to be so serious. Try injecting humor into your work environment following the guidance of this comedic duo:

1. **Use humor in your emails:** Ditch the stodgy corporate jargon and embrace a more human, approachable tone. You might try recalling moments of humor from phone calls with clients or use a "callback" joke in your follow-up emails. Consider including a playful "PS" in your messages as another option.
2. **Add levity to your bio or CV:** Inject a dash of humor and humility into your professional bio or CV. An example is an MBA who playfully describes his podcast as "affectionately described by my wife and two daughters as 'long, boring, and utterly devoid of substance.'" This approach signals confidence and arouses curiosity.
3. **Use humor to acknowledge mistakes or defuse tensions:** Instead of concluding an email with the customary "Sincerely," one individual lightened the atmosphere after being criticized for verbosity by writing, "In future, brevity."

(continued)

(continued)

4. **Get people in a creative mindset:** Encourage unconventional, whimsical ideas during brainstorming sessions. Google X's Captain of Moonshots, Astro Teller, encourages teams to conjure "the silliest, stupidest ideas." You may be chuckling, but I've witnessed its brilliant results.

5. **Create traditions out of organic moments of delight:** Transform unplanned moments of joy into enduring traditions. An example cited involves a Ford engineer who humorously likened a problem to "putting socks on a chicken." This inspired the tradition of gifting new hires and visitors with quirky chicken-themed socks.

Aaker and Bagdonas are well aware of the potential hazards of humor—occasionally, it can take an unfortunate turn into inappropriateness or offense. They generously provide valuable guidance for recognizing when a joke goes astray and offer insights on how to bounce back when humor falls flat. Their sage advice is simple: "As you move up the career ladder, make fun of others less, and yourself more."[17]

Let the Sparks Fly: How We Grow

Now that we've explored the challenges managers face during crises, where stress can be as intense as Bruce Banner's transformation into the Hulk, and the profound emotional and psychological impacts on both teams and leaders, take a moment to reflect on the following scripts to find your footing again and rekindle your inner spark as a manager.

Scripts for Managers and Teams

Managers:

- "I'm not feeling good about our earlier conversation. Can we chat about it?"
- "I've observed your strong skills in [area], and I'm confident that you can make a significant impact during these challenging times. How

can we more effectively harness these strengths in our present circumstances?"

- "I've noticed that you appear a bit disengaged from the team lately. What's preventing you from engaging more fully with your work and clicking with your coworkers? Is there anything I can do to help?"
- "Let's set a regular time for check-ins to ensure we're all on the same page and to address any concerns promptly."
- "I've noticed some signs of stress lately, such as [specifically name the signs]. How about we make some tweaks to address this?"
- "As we navigate these changes, I'm open to suggestions and new approaches from all of you.
- "I want to get your take on things, figure out what may slow you down, and explore solutions."
- "Your feedback is valuable. What's working, what's not? I'm all ears— promise, no eye rolls! I mean it—I can't solve what I don't know. Please share."

Teams:

- "I would like to discuss how I can continue working toward my career goals during these turbulent times."
- "I'm interested in developing [name specific skill] to contribute more effectively. Are there opportunities for this?"
- "I have some thoughts on [issue] that might help us navigate this period better. Can we discuss this in a quick brainstorm?"
- "I'd appreciate feedback on [task/project]. It will help me improve and adjust to our current situation."
- "I'm currently finding it challenging to engage with all the social and cultural challenges we face. Can we explore different options to express compassion that may be less taxing on our team?"
- "I faced [challenge] recently and addressed it by [solution]. I may need a backup or want to share this with you as it may impact my engagement with the team, and I would like to consider possible solutions."

- "I believe that if we collaborate on [project/task], we can achieve better results. What are your thoughts?"
- "With these new changes, I'm trying [strategy] to adapt. It might be useful for us."
- "I am implementing these (name them) strategies to manage stress and ensure my well-being. It's helping me stay productive and engaged, and I wanted to share these with you."

Remember: If tempers flare, take time to cool off. By remembering these points and using these scripts, you and your team can more effectively manage the emotional demands of modern workplaces, ensuring healthier personal and team dynamics.

4

Real Talk: Release Your Hungry Ghosts

"Why me?" I wondered out loud.

A colleague and I, both female C-suite executives, sat in our offices, deep in airing out our frustrations of the day. These sessions had morphed into a vital outlet for us, helping to shoulder the near-impossible demands of our jobs.

That day, our discussion gravitated toward a familiar sore point: the unequal burden we shouldered as women in the C-suite. Unlike some of our male colleagues, notorious for neglecting their duties or kicking up a fuss only to walk away like they hadn't just stirred the pot, guess who got to solve the resulting business mess and clean up the fallout from their drama? Yep—that responsibility invariably fell to us.

That afternoon, my patience was worn to its limit. I was inundated with a relentless flood of other people's issues, feeling like I was under a perpetual storm cloud—much like the one that eternally dampened Charlie Brown's spirits. The story I told myself was that I was the unlucky one who always drew the short straw. It was then that my colleague, more a friend in these trying times, offered a different perspective.

"Daisy, you'll find it easier to cope once you realize that work is filled with hungry ghosts," she said calmly.

"Say what?" I asked, my confusion evident.

She explained, "It's a concept from Buddhism about insatiable spirits. Everyone at work is a hungry ghost, always craving your time and attention. To keep your sanity, you need to set your boundaries and decide what you'll focus on and choose to avoid."

Her words were a sharp awakening for me, highlighting that it wasn't just about events occurring to me but how I allowed these dynamics to impact me.

In my career, as is the case for many women of color, I've often felt beaten into submission by abusive bosses and insecure colleagues. We've all been both victims and unwitting participants in systems that enforce our subjugation through deep-seated gendered racist biases, skewed power dynamics, and abusive behaviors. There I was, in a C-suite position, endowed with positional privilege and, importantly, with the responsibility to lead by example.

However, I found myself gripped by limiting beliefs, formed from past traumas and negative experiences. Her advice went beyond mere strategies for handling workplace dynamics; it served as a reminder that maintaining my inner peace was within my control, despite the unyielding demands of my role.

Let's face it: clinging to old ghosts, externally focused milestones, or past grievances doesn't just haunt you—it fries your circuits. So how can we manage our energy to fend off burnout and avoid becoming a living, breathing bundle of stress? How do we ease the grip of those psychological burdens that squeeze our serenity, happiness, and well-being?

In "The Transformation of Silence into Language and Action," from *Sister Outsider: Essays and Speeches*,[1] Audre Lorde wrote:

> We can learn to work and speak when we are afraid in the same way we have learned to work and speak when we are tired. For we have been socialized to respect fear more than our own needs for language and definition, and while we wait in silence for that final luxury of fearlessness, the weight of that silence will choke us.

In this chapter, I'll dive into a fusion of Eastern philosophies and modern-world insights. Get ready to tackle those hungry ghosts, those unfulfillable desires, underlying fears, and mental blocks that stealthily creep in, preventing us from becoming the leaders we want to be.

An Exploration into Hungry Ghosts at Work

Have you ever felt a sense of emptiness or unworthiness in your professional life? That's the hungry ghost's illusion.

The hungry ghost concept, from Asian cultures and religions like Buddhism and Taoism, describes beings with unending desires, often for material things or emotions. These ghosts are characterized by long, thin necks and swollen bellies, symbolizing their perpetual dissatisfaction and the consequences of greed and attachment.[2]

Hungry ghosts play tricks on us, and lead to burnout. They manifest in the relentless pursuit of money, growth, profit, status, or power—objectives that seldom result in fulfillment or happiness. They also appear as constant, unrelenting demands on our time and resources. People managers struggle to maximize team output, while employees often feel trapped in a never-ending cycle of trying to meet impossible performance goals, yet never truly pleasing anyone.

Every ambitious person who's convinced that the next rung on the corporate ladder is their golden ticket to a fatter paycheck, a fancier title, and a lifetime supply of power will likely end up disillusioned and drained upon realizing this belief is a fallacy.

Hey There, Self: Long Time No See

Leading a team can often feel like being a contestant on the comedy show *Whose Line Is It Anyway?* where guests improvise their way through a series of games and depend on audience suggestions. Every day is a juggling act of interpreting signals, deciding actions, aligning people and projects, influencing some while inevitably disappointing others, and then gearing up to repeat it all. All are highly dependent on the mandates and information you receive constantly. You're continually adapting based on endless streams of external input, and in this whirlwind, it's easy to lose your way.

We all have regrets, bad memories, and traumas. Understanding ourselves and how events in our lives have shaped us is crucial to recognizing the early signs of sliding down that slippery slope—whether that's the compulsion to respond to one more email, leaving notifications on, or that "one small thing" we tackle late at night. We need to set up guardrails to prevent burnout.

Remember the familiar flight safety instruction: "In the event of an emergency, please secure your own oxygen mask first before helping others." This is more than a safety tip; it's a metaphor for leadership. To lead effectively, with both courage and compassion, requires a deep understanding of our needs. Without this self-awareness, we risk our well-being and ability to guide and support those we lead.

How many times have you heard "centered" and "balanced" and thought of these as "woo-woo" words that only apply to other people?

Well, when life throws everything at you but the kitchen sink—and you know that as a leader you'll see it all!—these strategies from psychotherapist Annie Armstrong Miyao[3] to find clarity and peace come in handy:

- **Self Check-In:** Begin by tuning into your mind and body. Recognize your motivations. Conduct a body scan to notice physical and emotional states. Acknowledge your mood and thought patterns without judgment.
- **Consider Your Needs:** Shift focus from "What do I need to do?" to "What do I need?" This might include basic internal needs like hydration or emotional needs like social interaction.
- **List Your Values:** Write down what matters most to you, what activities bring joy, and what you would do if you had complete freedom. Use these reflections to identify and highlight your top 10 values. To build your values list, she suggests asking these questions:
  - What matters to me?
  - At the end of the day, I always feel good when I. . .
  - If I got to spend one month doing as I pleased, I would. . .

Like any psychotherapist or a good friend, Armstrong Miyao stresses the importance of setting boundaries to preserve your serenity. To ensure that the boundaries you establish align with your priorities, she recommends reflecting on the following considerations:

- Are the choices I'm making ones that honor my values?
- Reflect on a time when you prioritized others over yourself: What motivated your actions? What aspects were draining for you? Where did pressure originate for you? Any neglected needs? How did you energetically approach those tasks? What was your mindset?

- When advocating for yourself: What boundaries would you establish for yourself? What does offering grace look like for you?

Understanding what matters to you and determining the proper boundaries to set is like building muscle; it requires time, patience, and consistent practice. If you're not ready to answer all the questions now, that's OK. Keep in mind these subtle prompts that you control your time, energy, and joy, which can help reduce your susceptibility to burnout.

Turning Unhappiness into Happiness

We all face setbacks, disappointments, and failures. What if we could transform these moments when the prospect of what lies ahead makes us want to hide away into powerful lessons of happiness and gratitude? Author and professor Arthur Brooks suggests a unique method: maintaining a failure and disappointment journal.[4] This technique isn't about dwelling on the negative but actively managing and learning from it.

Here's how it works: Whenever you encounter a setback or disappointment, you write it down. This recording allows you to confront and manage the situation rather than letting it control you. You jot down the event and what you learned and set a one-month and six-month reminder.

Picture this: You've just nailed a presentation, or so you thought, but then your manager hits you with criticism that feels like a bucket of cold water. Ouch. Naturally, you're gutted. But here's a twist: instead of letting this memory fester in your mind, whip out your journal and scribble it down.

A month later, revisit the entry and reflect on what you've learned from that experience. Now, with the benefit of hindsight, you may realize that the initial sting of the criticism faded quicker than you expected. Something that felt devastating at the moment feels less so. Roll on six months, and that same journal entry has another surprise. That stinging critique? It was the nudge you needed to realize you and your job were like oil and water—not the best mix. Fast forward a bit, and you're now in a role that's more "you," more rewarding, more. . .everything.

(continued)

(*continued*)

Throughout my career, I've experienced crushing professional setbacks, the kind that bring you to your knees and confine you to bed for days. Once, when I was deeply upset about missing out on what seemed like a once-in-a-lifetime role, my leadership coach, Rha Goddess, soothed me with these words: "Don't see it as rejection, but as protection." She then encouraged me, as she often did, to journal about the experience, suggesting that it was a preparation for something even better.[5] Arthur Brooks echoes this sentiment, proposing that a healthier perspective on failure turns setbacks into learning opportunities. Every mishap and "why me?" moment becomes a golden ticket to a happier, wiser version of yourself. So the next time life hurls lemons at you, grab your journal and start scribbling—who knows, you might just draft the masterplan for your next career adventure!

Self-Care Like You Mean It

If we're depleted, we're unable to lead others effectively.

Have you ever found yourself rolling your eyes at a team member's suggestion, only to regret the public embarrassment you caused them? Or yourself? Or stormed out of your boss's office, fuming over an ever-growing checklist, berating yourself for not asking to reprioritize your workload? Maybe you've gossiped about a colleague's last-minute requests instead of directly and kindly suggesting ways they could improve their time management.

If these scenarios sound familiar, you're not alone—I've been there too. And each time, I've regretted letting my exhaustion and tendency to prioritize others cloud my judgment about how I want to show up at work. When we're worn out, we can't be our most effective, courageous, and discerning selves.

In her book *Real Self-Care*, psychiatrist Pooja Lakshmin emphasizes that true self-care means holding people and pain together.[6] She critiques the superficial, commercialized version of self-care—what she calls "faux self-care"—which only leads to further exhaustion and disillusionment. However, for those of us living inside raging firestorms that burn us to a crisp, there's hope, starting with prioritizing our well-being. This form of real self-care, especially crucial for women, as Lakshmin notes in her book, is the key to thriving amidst life's relentless demands.

Here are Lakshmin's essential principles:

- **Self-Care Requires Boundaries and Moving Past Guilt:** Mastering the art of saying no and establishing clear boundaries is crucial. It's about distinguishing between the needs of others and your own.
- **Self-Care Means Treating Yourself with Compassion:** Ditch the self-sacrificing martyr mindset that leads to resentment. Instead, prioritize kindness toward yourself.
- **Self-Care Brings You Closer to Yourself:** The aim is to align with your core values, beliefs, and desires. Self-care brings you closer to understanding and fulfilling these aspects of yourself.
- **Self-Care Is an Assertion of Power:** Embrace and leverage your capacity for change. Self-care is a powerful assertion of your agency and ability to influence your life positively.

Lakshmin describes burnout as "societal betrayal at its most disturbing level." She emphasizes that the prevalent focus on "fixing the people" misses the mark. Instead, she argues, the systems in our lives and workplaces are failing us. This systemic failure is most conspicuously manifested as burnout. Lakshmin astutely observes that the societal game is rigged, particularly in a patriarchal context. Women are disproportionately saddled with the mental load—the cognitive and emotional labor associated with managing a household—and are subjected to a series of contradictory expectations. These pressures, she notes, drive women toward superficial forms of self-care in a desperate attempt to find a solution to their overwhelming challenges.

Understanding real self-care involves recognizing it's not merely about superficial remedies but confronting deeper systemic issues. The first step in this process is identifying detrimental elements in our lives, such as external pressures or circumstances that sap our energy. However, awareness alone is insufficient. It's equally vital to take control of our lives proactively. This means setting self-boundaries that declare that we matter, steering clear of demands likely to deplete us and making deliberate choices that nourish and enhance our well-being.

What is your cognitive overload? Sociologist and researcher Allison Daminger, PhD, describes women's cognitive (or mental) load in household management as "anticipating needs, identifying options for filling them, making decisions, and monitoring progress."[7] Remarkably, this mirrors the daily responsibilities of a people manager!

Self-care isn't just one thing like unwinding on a massage table. It's a dynamic, continuous process that can help you tune into your mental and emotional states to understand when to take a step back from anxiety-inducing situations or reengage with others to thaw what has become stagnant or frozen within us.

It demands a deep and honest examination of our lives to discern what's working and what isn't. This understanding is pivotal in addressing and healing broken aspects, not just temporarily easing the strain with surface-level fixes.

Like many others, I often wrestle with the guilt or hesitation of prioritizing self-care. Since childhood, I've internalized a narrative that sometimes it's simpler to put the needs of others before my own rather than articulate them. However, whose comfort am I sacrificing most by adhering to this mindset? The answer is mine. This approach lays the foundation for two significant components of burnout: resentment and exhaustion.

While I initially saw typical self-care activities like facials, massages, manicures, and pedicures as indulgences, I now recognize them as essential forms of relaxation and consciously include them routinely in my well-being regimen.

In my personal life, this is how I protect my well-being:

- **Selective RSVPs:** I politely decline to social invitations or advisory board requests that would overburden my schedule, no matter how appealing or meaningful they are.
- **Non-Negotiable Exercise:** My workout time is sacred and immovable on my calendar. My exercise routine is my pharmacy, essential for my physical and mental health.
- **Communicating with My Partner:** I've learned to be upfront with my husband, especially when I come home exhausted. If I need a moment to recharge before discussing his day, I gently communicate that need.

At work, these are practices that help me maintain balance and focus:

- **Scheduled "Me Time":** I block out chunks of time in my work calendar specifically for myself. During these breaks, I might exercise, do breath work, go for a leisurely walk, or take a moment to close my eyes and relax, especially in between back-to-back meetings.
- **Thoughtful Communication:** I avoid the urge to respond immediately to emails or voicemails. Instead, I wait a few hours, responding when I feel more energized and can give a more thoughtful and considerate reply.
- **Intentionally Responding to "Do You Have 15 Minutes?":** When asked for a quick chat, and I genuinely don't have those spare 15 minutes—knowing it'll make me late for my next meeting or result in joining unprepared—I tactfully ask if it can wait. If it's not urgent, we schedule a time that suits us both. It's about balancing responsiveness with managing my schedule effectively.

Recognizing that my time, energy, and attention are limited resources is an ongoing process. Actively choosing activities that bring joy and possibility is not just self-care but a potent form of leadership that kicks hungry ghosts to the curb. Such a mindset can revolutionize how we guide others and motivate those around us to embrace similar practices in their own lives.

Say Thank You to the Good Stuff and to Yourself

As children, most of us are taught to say thank you to the people who open a door for us, provide a service, or give us gifts. As people leaders, we know that it's a sign of respect to thank those you work with for a job well done or going out of their way to help you out with a last-minute project.

But how many times do we offer gratitude for the good things in our lives, the people we lead and who lead us, and to ourselves?

In his TED Talk, Brother David Steindl-Rast, a monk and scholar, highlights a universal truth: our shared pursuit of happiness stems from gratitude.[8]

Gratitude isn't just about feeling thankful; it's a transformative force. It shifts us from fear to peace, reducing tendencies toward aggression. A grateful mindset fosters a sense of abundance, not scarcity, prompting us to share and connect. It helps us appreciate the uniqueness in others, fostering respect and harmony.

A gratitude-centric mindset boosts happiness and optimism, frequently transforming our outlook on life. Rather than dwelling on what's missing, it encourages us to value what we have and look forward to what's yet to be revealed.

Harvard Health Publishing reveals some compelling benefits of gratitude: just a weekly gratitude journal entry can increase optimism by 15%, workplace gratitude boosts employee productivity, and expressing gratitude in relationships enhances positive feelings and open communication.[9]

Embracing gratitude is like arming yourself with a secret weapon for a mental makeover. It's a powerful antidote to the hungry ghosts of scarcity and dissatisfaction that often haunt our daily lives. Remember, there's no one-size-fits-all in this journey; the trick is to discover the gratitude practices that resonate with you.

Here are some practical ideas to kickstart your gratitude practice, no frills needed. (Please try not to side-eye me until you've tried it):

- **Kickstart Your Day with Gratitude:** In a practice inspired by leadership coach Zander Grashow, start your day by listing three things you're grateful for.[10] Before leaving bed, take three deep breaths and think of these things. It might be as simple as family members, but this small act can bring a smile to your face and set a tone of contentment and appreciation for the day.
- **Journal Gratitude:** No need for elaborate journals. Grab any notebook or use your phone's Notes app. Regularly list three to five things you're thankful for, big or small—a cozy morning coffee or a meaningful chat. Arthur Brooks's idea fits here: note down challenging experiences and later reflect on the positive takeaways. It's all about recognizing and appreciating the good, whether obvious or hidden.
- **Express Gratitude:** Expressing thanks doesn't require lengthy prose. A simple, heartfelt message often means the most. Annually, I reach out to those who've influenced me—mentors from the past or recent acquaintances—to express my gratitude. Whether through a brief email or a handwritten card, the goal is genuine expression, not length. This practice is about brightening someone's day and acknowledging the positive impact others have had in our lives.

- **Reflect with Gratitude:** Whether journaling or sending a weekly note to your team, reflecting on what it means to be a good leader can bolster your mental health. Sharing your thoughts and experiences, even mistakes, with your team models vulnerability and encourages a positive affirmation culture.

Incorporating Gratitude into Team Meetings:
- **Unwind Before the Grind:** Kick off meetings with a calming moment using apps like Calm, Headspace, or Oura. It's like giving your brain a mini spa treatment before diving into the agenda.
- **Rotate Gratitude on the Agenda:** Spice up meetings with a gratitude round. Each session, a different team member gets to share something personal that they wish to celebrate. It's like a happiness lottery, but everyone wins!
- **Shake Things Up:** Tired of the same old meeting routine? Throw in something fresh, like an improv session. It not only breaks monotony but also enhances brain neuroplasticity, alleviates stress, and builds resilience.
- **Connect-the-Dots Chats:** Regular heart-to-hearts with your team can be a game-changer. Apart from my one-on-ones with direct reports, I schedule quarterly meetings with everyone on my team. This allows me to connect with junior members who often are closest to the pain points in organizations. It's like collecting all the pieces of a puzzle—every bit counts!

Find Your Inner Silence

At a CHRO retreat hosted by BetterUp in the fall of 2023, a coaching, mentorship and content platform company, research professor and bestselling author Brené Brown observed, "We're emotional beings who, on occasion, think."[11]

While that's true, this statement can be a tough pill to swallow for those who pride themselves on being "rational thinkers." But I've also learned that, as Eastern philosophy teaches, our bodies possess an innate wisdom far deeper than we often acknowledge. By embracing and surrendering to this deep-seated wisdom, and letting go and trusting our natural instincts, we can release emotional constraints and prevent burnout.

If you've ever practiced yoga and wanted to roll your eyes whenever you heard someone say, "Be gentle on yourself. Observe the pain and breathe through it," I've been you. But in the spirit of trying new things, I've dabbled with several yoga practices from Ashtanga to Bikram yoga—all admittedly commercialized Western interpretations of this ancient wisdom—and I've discovered they help me reset, quiet my restless mind, and leave me feeling genuinely better. Who knew those clichéd phrases could hold some truth?

For instance, during an Ayurvedic and yoga wellness retreat, I found myself under the guidance of Suyash, a yogi whose calmness seemed to still the air around him.[12] He opened my eyes to the depths of yoga and meditation, revealing how much I had misunderstood these ancient practices. Initially, I had ventured to this retreat seeking a simple escape, a chance to relax and recharge. Little did I know I was about to embark on a journey of unlearning, rediscovery, and releasing my hungry ghosts.

I learned that addressing health imbalances, including burnout, starts with building a deeper connection with the body and mind, and the way I've been "doing yoga" was, as Pooja Lakshmin would say, "faux yoga." Suyash and his colleagues further taught me that our mental clutter—fear, anxiety, distrust, and turmoil—can spiral into physical ailments, burnout included.

In a one-on-one meditation session during the retreat, Suyash and I shared a laugh over my struggles. "I try, but the monkeys in my head get in the way." I admitted. The monkeys in my head, clearly, were my hungry ghosts playing tricks on me. Suyash smiled knowingly, saying, "Being aware of the monkeys is good," adding, "Sometimes, you just have to choose which monkey to arm with the sword." Right, I can decide which thoughts deserve my attention and which ones to let go of. But why is it so hard?

When he learned of my role as a chief people officer, Suyash observed, "Ah, working with humans is difficult work. You must find a balance between your head space and heart space to discern what thoughts you allow in and not." He pointed to my head and then my heart, indicating that while he believed I was fine with the intellectual parts of my job, I also needed to cultivate empathy for myself and others. Harmonizing these two aspects, my chakras, he suggested, was essential for offering balanced guidance and care.

Suyash recommended focusing on my inner silence as a path to this goal. I giggled. Silence is not my thing. He proposed that through silent meditation, I could learn to observe and gently redirect the restless thoughts that cluttered my mind. This technique, he explained, would be instrumental in helping me find the peace and balance crucial for living a healthy life and enhance my capacity to lead others with care and wisdom.

Suyash's insights on balance echo the Western idea of self-regulation. Leading with a sense of balance allows us to steer others through difficulties without succumbing to fear or anxiety—those unyielding "monkeys" in our minds. It's about listening to the right voices—your inner voice of truth—versus the louder voices yelling at us over the loudspeaker that we're bad managers and our performance blows. And it's about looking ahead down the road to avoid the speed traps that lead to burnout. Those are the voices that deplete us.

As leaders, we must work hardest at understanding our own emotional responses to stave off burnout. We can create healthier and more productive workplaces by being more attuned to what's happening around us and responding thoughtfully rather than reacting impulsively or ignoring the uninvited ghosts that creep in.

Leave It There

"Leave it there."

I received a simple yet powerful lesson from an Ayurvedic doctor during an eye-opening consultation.[13] After briefly examining my tongue, she pegged me as a Pitha overload—essentially, a walking fireball. When asked about the source of my stress, my immediate answer was "work." Her response was simple: "If you don't leave it, it builds a fire in you, and it can burn you."

Think about it: How often do we drag office drama home? How frequently do we allow a harsh email to ruin our dinner or brood over being misunderstood or overlooked in a meeting? The doctor's advice was clear: Leave. It. There.

I've embraced "Leave It There" as a mantra, a protective shield against emotional imbalance. And trust me, this is not just talk; it's a practical approach to managing stress, releasing self-criticism, and helping us lead from a place of harmony and joy.

Because isn't that what we all want? Even more than what the hungry ghost is after?

Dodging Burnout with Ancient Ayurvedic Wisdom

The "Ashtanga Hridayam," a revered text in the ancient Indian science of Ayurveda, offers a wealth of knowledge on everything health related. This isn't your typical ancient scripture health manual; it's more like a life coach in maintaining balance in all facets of life. It advises everything from your morning routine to what and how you should eat.[14]

Now, let's be real. Applying Ayurvedic wisdom to today's boardroom battles and email avalanches might sound like mixing oil with water, but hear me out. In this burnout-infested corporate jungle, I've found many relevant and beneficial insights into facing the stressors of today's workplace.

- **Listen to Your Body's Natural Rhythms:** Running on three hours of sleep and a vat of coffee? Ayurveda says that's a highway to Burnoutville.
- **Eat Wise, Energize:** Poor eating habits lead to physical and mental fatigue. That midday slump might be your diet yelling for an intervention.
- **Move It or Lose It:** Ayurveda's take? Overexertion or a sedentary lifestyle can both lead to crash and burnout.
- **Mind Matters:** Mental and emotional health isn't just for Gen Z. It's central in Ayurveda and crucial for dodging that burnout bullet.
- **Stress Less:** Chronic stress due to imbalances in life is like junk food for your soul; leaning on healthy coping strategies is a must.
- **Self-Care Isn't Selfish:** Neglecting "me time" is a no-no in Ayurveda and a yes-yes to burnout.
- **Balance Is Key:** All work and no rest? Ayurveda called it centuries ago—that's a recipe for a meltdown.
- **Ditch the Toxic Vibes:** Whether it's people or places or you finding fault in others, if it drains you, Ayurveda's advice is to let it go.
- **Listen to Your Body's Whispers:** A sniffle here, a headache there—Ayurveda says not to ignore those early SOS signals.
- **Change Is the Only Constant:** Not syncing your lifestyle with life's changes? Ayurveda warns this might tip your balance off.

Now, of course I don't have an Ayurvedic degree on my wall. But I've listened to, absorbed, and tried to weave practitioners' interpretations into the tapestry of my daily hustle. And you know what? These age-old pearls of wisdom are shockingly relevant to our modern-day scramble. You don't have to do everything all at once. When I learned, yet again, that my habit of late-night TV watching was messing with my chakras, I enlisted my husband and daughter to kindly remind me to let go of electronics after 9:30 p.m., even if I was on deadline. My sleep patterns improved significantly.

Why not blend some of these ancient practices with your modern lifestyle? It could lead to a holistic strategy to sidestep burnout and keep our heads above water in this whirlwind of life.

What Do You Truly Want?

I've found that we often neglect to ask ourselves the most crucial question: "What do I truly want?" This reflective question goes beyond the obvious societal norms or the superficial expectations of others. It requires us to dig into our deepest personal desires and aspirations. A therapist once guided me through this reflective process, encouraging me to examine whether my actions were aligned with my desires. She asked me to consider a straightforward yet profound question: "Is this response moving me closer to what I genuinely want or need?" This query is universally applicable, whether deciding how to respond to a nasty email or considering taking on new work responsibilities. It helps evaluate if our actions are aligned with what we most need or merely an attempt to impress others.

Sitting in a spacious conference room at round tables alongside fellow board members, with autumn leaves descending outside, the CEO of a prominent enterprise candidly discussed a series of challenges the organization had encountered in the past week. With a solemn demeanor and a tone of gravity, he recounted a succession of work-related trials. He stressed the diligence with which his team approached each evolving situation, prioritizing careful consideration and adherence to guiding principles. He repeatedly assured us of his commitment to informing us about the ongoing progress.

The expectation at work has always been to stay silent when you're not OK, to ignore or dismiss it instead of accepting that not everything is within our power to manage or control.

Moved by the weight of his words and the emotions he conveyed, I spoke up. "You have an impossible job, and I understand the difficulty of making imperfect decisions. Please let us know how we can support you, and remember to grant yourself the grace to acknowledge that you won't get everything right all the time."

In response, he reframed his perspective, saying, "Thank you. I consider myself to have the best job in the world, but sometimes it can be challenging."

Following that, he shared that he was due to take a sabbatical as per organizational policy. With a touch of self-deprecation, he mumbled about how everyone else had taken sabbaticals, but he had never done so in his entire career. He then sheepishly stated his intention to take one in the upcoming months and sought the board's support. In a unanimous display of agreement, we all nodded in approval.

He went on to describe his sabbatical plan: "Due to the high-profile projects currently underway, I won't disconnect fully. I plan to check my emails perhaps once a week, address time-sensitive campaigns, and remain available as needed."

Promptly, hands shot up around the room, with board members expressing their concerns. We voiced our opinions one after another, saying, "Now, this is not a true sabbatical. You deserve a complete break. What we need is a comprehensive plan to ensure your responsibilities are adequately covered during your absence. This will provide your staff and key stakeholders with a clear level of understanding. But most importantly, by not taking a proper sabbatical, you inadvertently message your staff that they shouldn't either. Let's work together to find a solution that aligns with your goals, supports your team and ongoing projects, and encourages a genuine sabbatical experience."

As a people leader and advisor to other managers and executives, I often notice two common stress responses among high-performing individuals, particularly those in leadership roles. This observation, confirmed through numerous discussions with leadership coaches and therapists, highlights that people either exert excessive control over their surroundings or avoid responsibilities as a defense mechanism. Both approaches lead to strained team dynamics and personal stress. Over-functioning, while it may temporarily reduce anxiety, often results in burnout due to taking on too many responsibilities. On the other hand, under-functioning, characterized by avoiding risks and relying on others to do the work, can diminish personal growth and effectiveness. In this case, this CEO was experiencing burnout from over-functioning and was having a hard time asking for the help he needed to regulate and come back healthier and stronger for his team.

In this scenario, imagine if the CEO had taken the time to confront his hungry ghosts—those internal narratives limiting his perception of creating a fulfilling work life. Such self-reflection might have enabled him to assess whether his approach to the sabbatical aligned with his wellness goals. This process would ensure his decisions were not just reactionary but intentionally crafted to foster his well-being and peace of mind.

Getting Unstuck Is the New Normal

When we find ourselves stuck, it might feel like our hard-earned skills and lessons aren't working for us. Don't be hard on yourself if you're trying to motivate others but are struggling to self-motivate. This is a common, temporary phase, especially for people leaders. Managers often feel that they've been left to fend for themselves while juggling daily challenges. Remember, you're not alone.

Trends like "quiet quitting" and "quiet firing" signal a more profound, ongoing crisis. These phenomena aren't just passing occurrences; they point to fundamental problems in work culture and personal fulfillment. Employees who disengage from their roles, doing only what's required and pulling back from extra efforts, often do it in response to unacknowledged hard work, lack of trust in leadership, or poor compensation. On the other hand, poor management practices, like subtly pushing employees toward resignation through insufficient support, ignoring opportunities for promotions, or creating hostile and unjust work conditions, can lead to employees feeling devalued and alienated.

In *The Burnout Challenge: Managing People's Relationships with Their Jobs*, authors Christina Maslach and Michael P. Leiter delve into the intricacies of workplace burnout.[15] They highlight three core aspects: exhaustion, cynicism, and inefficiency, and how they culminate in burnout. As leaders, recognizing and addressing these underlying challenges is essential in navigating the current landscape without letting it deplete us and our teams.

These trends are more than individual grievances; they highlight deep-rooted problems within organizational structures. Managers with severely limited bandwidth are sometimes unable to offer any support at all. While promoting balance, clear communication, and opportunities for growth are essential, these efforts fall short without a fundamentally human-centric work approach that prioritizes employee well-being, encourages open dialogue, and values personal satisfaction.

Fixing deep-rooted systemic workplace failures like gender and racial biases is no overnight task. But we can start by not letting them rent space in our heads. Releasing ourselves from external pressures and self-imposed expectations is possible. That's where mindfulness techniques come into play—think breathing with intention, stretching (and not just pre-workouts), and cutting ourselves some slack.

The key to getting unstuck is often to quiet the mind and listen to our inner voice, especially during crisis. This introspection and valuing of our insights can be a guiding light during turbulent times.

Believe Your People

If your employee tells you they're burned out, believe them. Workplace stress has been linked to management practices, workload distribution, and interpersonal conflicts, among other factors. While it might not appear to be classic burnout, their experience is real and deserves your attention.

In her article "When Your Employee Tells You They're Burned Out," Noémie Le Pertel emphasizes the importance of being ready when employees express burnout.[16] Being burnout-ready means being prepared to ask questions that can help explore the potential stressors they might face either at work or in their personal life. In your one-on-one meetings, you might want to consider asking:

- When did you feel most productive and connected to your work this week?
- What gets in the way of a good and productive workday for you?
- How do you channel joy, hope, and optimism on the worst days?

- Have your feelings about your coworkers and work changed at all in the past year?
- What support do you need to be your best, personally and professionally? Suggest specific options for those unsure of what to request: Would extending timelines or deadlines help? What about addressing conflicts with coworkers, reevaluating priorities, changing work assignments or your physical workspace?

These questions can unearth potential organizational issues or personal concerns about their performance or the purpose of their work. They can illuminate various emotional, social, or physical challenges such as fatigue, anxiety, frequent illnesses, or caregiving duties that may be influencing their well-being and productivity. Additionally, they can expose whether aspects like workload, team dynamics, personal circumstances, or other factors affect their energy levels.

Forgive Yourself and Others

I'll never forget the day when a young woman walked into my office for a "get to know you" interview as part of her onboarding process. Right from the start, it was clear that she was intelligent, ambitious, and direct. As I began offering insights into the organization, she asked a question that surprised me: "Who is your best friend here?"

I was momentarily stunned.

While I could rely on a support network outside of work composed of friends across various industries, I realized I didn't have anyone in the office who I could quickly ask, "Do you see what I'm seeing?" or turn to for advice. It made me wonder who my trusted colleagues were, those who could prevent me from making a social misstep or offer reassurance with a message like "It wasn't your fault; he's angry at everyone today." It was a feeling of loneliness I hadn't anticipated.

As a woman of color frequently in the situation Deepa Purushotham refers to as "The First, the Few, the Only" in her book, especially in workplace settings, I found it challenging to lower my guard and establish trustful relationships at work.[17] Although I have formed lasting relationships, there have been times when my willingness to be vulnerable was turned against me.

There was the time a colleague I had turned to for solace, sharing personal doubts about an impending promotion, unfortunately disclosed this information to her boss and mine, suggesting I might not be prepared for the forthcoming opportunity. My boss shared this betrayal as a lesson in choosing confidants wisely. He retained faith in my capabilities and entrusted me with the new opportunity.

I learned my lesson. Moreover, I excelled in my expanded role.

However, sometimes we must absorb these lessons without allowing ourselves to become hardened. Counting on strong, trusting connections with my peers and those reporting to me has continued to be an essential survival strategy, despite occasional setbacks. At times, leading people can feel so isolating that building friendships becomes difficult, resulting in profound loneliness.

According to "The Cost of Loneliness: Women, Work & The Invisible Force That's Undermining Them As They Rise," a research study carried out by TheL.ist, Berlin Cameron and Benenson Strategy Group:

- 53% of women report that their job leads to loneliness, primarily from isolation, a lack of support, and the need to mask their true selves at the workplace.
- Nearly 70% of women report being unsupported, while 51% express isolation at work.
- The experience of loneliness or isolation becomes more pronounced as women progress in their careers.
- Women of color face an even more pronounced sense of isolation, exacerbated by a lack of respect, with 27% expressing that they do not feel respected by those under their supervision.[18]

Kindness, like self-care, starts with oneself. Sure, but releasing self-criticism, righteousness, victimization, and ego are hard to do. We frequently become our most severe critics in our unyielding quest for success and perfection. The internal dialogues I most need to silence are the ones filled with self-rebuke: "Daisy, you botched that talk with Henny. She needed your ears, not your solutions." Or "Really? That was your best response to

Mel's questions?" These voices amplify my self-doubt and impede my journey toward kinder self-perception and more balanced self-assessment.

One of the most powerful yet often neglected tools in leadership is the practice of self-forgiveness. Far more than a mere act of kindness, self-forgiveness is essential for alleviating stress and preventing burnout. It allows leaders to acknowledge missteps while moving forward without the burden of self-recrimination.

What Is This Self-Forgiveness You Speak About?

Self-forgiveness is the intentional process of letting go of negative feelings directed toward oneself for past actions or mistakes. It's when you say no to the loud voices that tell you you're worthless and remind yourself of your worth. Here's what the steps look like:

1. **Acknowledge the Mistake:** "Megan, I'm sorry that I jumped to delivering solutions instead of spending more time listening to what you really needed."
2. **Learn from It:** Take a moment to check yourself the next time you're in a one-to-one meeting to make sure you don't jump to solve mode.
3. **Move Forward Without Self-Imposed Guilt or Resentment:** Be grateful for the lesson and leave it there. "OK, I learned my lesson. I will do better next time."

To be clear, this practice does not mean excusing poor behavior but understanding and accepting that we are fallible and can learn and grow.

So how does self-forgiveness help us release the choke of stress? Holding onto self-blame can perpetuate a state of continuous stress, which often manifests in physical symptoms like insomnia, fatigue, and a weakened immune system—all potential precursors to burnout. By practicing self-forgiveness, we can escape this harmful cycle. As I've mentioned, drawing from Arthur Brooks's concept of a "failure journal," this approach enables us to see failures as opportunities for growth rather than as stains on our character or abilities.

To release our grip on the hungry ghosts that deplete us, we need to understand our reaction patterns and recognize that our behaviors often stem from deep-seated fears and anxieties. By identifying these habitual responses, we can consciously choose actions that better serve our needs and goals rather than those that drain us.

Each decision we make and action we take carries weight and impact. By cultivating greater mindfulness of our emotions and energy flow, we can make choices that alleviate our stress and propel us toward achieving our leadership aspirations and well-being.

Let the Sparks Fly: How We Grow

This chapter explored how leadership is often a journey marked by missteps and challenges, integral to personal growth. Addressing our "hungry ghosts"—our fears and mental blocks—requires understanding our emotional triggers, learning from our mistakes, and focusing on self-awareness, self-care, and self-forgiveness. This includes establishing boundaries and being kind to ourselves, essential practices for preventing burnout. Such self-management enhances our well-being and equips us to provide better support and leadership for others. Let's now turn our attention to some scripts to help you rekindle your inner spark as a manager:

Scripts for Managers and Teams

Managers:

- **Morning:** "Today, I will withhold from judging myself and others, honor my limits and focus on what aligns with my highest priorities. It's OK not to meet every demand."
- **Midday:** "Taking a moment to tune in with my feelings, check my social battery, and tweak things to dial down the stress is essential for my well-being."
- **Evening:** "I did my best today. I celebrate my wins, learn from my mistakes, and move forward with a grateful mindset."

Teams:

- **Morning Huddle:** "Let's start by sharing something we're grateful for and focus on goals that we can achieve this week, supporting each other."
- **Midday Reminder:** "If you're feeling swamped, let's have a chat so I can see where we might adjust workloads or expectations, and tackle stress together."

- **End of Day:** "I appreciate our achievements and the opportunities we have for improvements. Remember, our shared success and well-being is our strength."

Pro tip: Ask a colleague or your manager to help you stick to your boundaries. Say out loud, "I'm committed to being more mindful of my capacity and commitments but I have to work at it. Would you help me maintain these boundaries?" Think of it like having a personal bouncer for your "no."

These scripts aim to establish a culture of empathy and shared understanding within teams. They encourage recognizing and respecting personal and collective limits, creating a safe space for expressing needs, and addressing challenges. This supportive atmosphere is key to mitigating burnout and fostering a healthy, productive work environment.

PART III

Leading Through an Inferno

5

Hang in There: Leading Through the Diversity, Equity, Inclusion, and Belonging Firestorm

"I'm exhausted from managing everyone's emotions!"

On a crisp autumn day, five women of color, all executives, gathered around a dinner table in a New York City restaurant. These dinners had been a treasured ritual for over a decade, serving as a refuge through the ups and downs of our careers, including periods of burnout and triumph. This evening, we were celebrating a birthday and, in keeping with our tradition, we exchanged stories ranging from managing the challenges of raising children from middle school to college, leading teams, and our concerns about the tumultuous state of the world.

As one of four seasoned diversity, equity, and inclusion (DEI) experts shared this comment, there was a collective, knowing nod around the table.

"It's truly draining," another voiced, capturing a sentiment we all understood and silently acknowledged with another round of empathetic nods.

We had all ventured into our fields fueled by the ambition of shaping more inclusive and equitable workplaces than the ones we first experienced. We were bound by our shared career journeys through predominantly white, male-dominated corporate landscapes, where feelings of being undervalued were common, and adapting to others' comfort often meant suppressing our voices and protecting our well-being. Each of us had repeatedly assumed the challenging role of voicing hard truths, familiar with the difficulties confronting a system that often blocks underrepresented individuals.

As we climbed our respective career ladders, leading increasingly larger teams, we learned the nuanced art of inclusive people management. We understood the significance of actively listening to our teams and valuing their voices, identities, and overall well-being while achieving business goals.

But this time felt different.

Our energy was depleted from tackling long-standing operational and systemic challenges and the draining effort of handling a wide array of emotions in our environment. A combination of factors further intensified this:

- The persistent effects of the pandemic
- Rising social tensions
- Market instability
- Changing customer demands and employee expectations
- Backlash against DEI programs and policies

We found ourselves steering through the apprehensions of executives anxious about losing their influence and managers struggling with their new complex responsibilities, all while addressing the persistent calls from employees demanding their voices be heard. This relentless emotional labor was exceptionally draining.

"Retention" was the buzzword, but it was misplaced energy. Organizations continued to shield those in power, opting for quick-fix solutions, seemingly to bridge to the next economic cycle. Meanwhile, workers and other stakeholders like clients, audiences, and shareholders vocally demanded substantive change. Adding to this complexity were changes in the legal landscape and cutbacks in corporate investments, which posed challenges against DEI initiatives.

For the first time, we confronted a DEI crisis that left us unsure of the path forward.

In this chapter, I'll share stories from the front lines of DEI work, whether you're a DEI practitioner, a manager accountable for your team's DEI achievements, or someone deeply invested in these issues. I'll also explore self-preservation strategies, a vital aspect for sustaining DEI efforts despite obstacles.

DEI: Is It for Real?

Years ago, I was in a sprawling conference room with DEI leaders from Silicon Valley's top tech firms. One of our peers had recently come under fire for their diversity efforts, and as a precaution against leaks, we were all advised to bring along our communications partners. What should have been a meeting of bright, committed minds crafting progressive solutions turned into hours of a cautious exchange of strategies— sufficient to seem cooperative but too guarded to foster progressive collaboration.

At one point, unable to contain my frustration, I broke the tension. "We're all here walking on eggshells because of human mistakes in one of our organizations. We're each secretly relieved not to be the one in the hot seat. But the truth is, any of us could be in that spot next. Why not drop the pretenses and have an honest conversation about collaborating effectively?" My words broke some ice, drawing smiles and nods of agreement. However, the underlying corporate caution and a pervasive culture of silence impeded the progress I believe we all hoped for. It was a stark reminder of how status quo corporate pressures, even among practitioners, can derail our efforts, weakening our collective force.

Which is to say, DEI is very real.

The discussion about whether DEI initiatives are superficial and the competency of their leaders has long been a point of resistance. This debate was sharply accentuated in the summer of 2023 when several prominent Black DEI executives left their positions in Hollywood. These high-profile departures ignited industry-wide discussions, leading to the question "Is DEI dead?" Fueling this debate was a LinkedIn post by Walt Geer, the chief experience design officer at VMLY&R, titled "DEI is Dead. Prove Me Wrong." The post rapidly gained widespread attention and sparked a broad range of responses, from strong affirmations of the ongoing necessity for DEI work to critiques of performative actions and demands for tangible, measurable change.

This public debate has one thing clear: the work of DEI is a roller coaster. This arduous work often leaves DEI managers, their teams and managers burned out with hope deflated as they, too, experience microaggressions, resistance, and toxicity.

Jeanelle English, the former executive VP of Impact and Inclusion at the Movie Academy, was one of the Black executives who left their positions the summer of 2023, just a year into her role. She penned a column for the *LA Times* titled "Former Oscars Diversity Chief on 'Micro- and Macro-Aggressions' That Led to Exit,"[1] where she openly discussed the fear and scarcity mindset that influenced her decision to resign:

As a result, I became the recipient of a steady flux of micro- and macro-aggressions. I anticipated and grew accustomed to being regularly challenged, publicly and privately. I felt the pressure of remaining thoughtful, poised and *articulate* while coaching, counseling and responding to the needs of my colleagues also from marginalized communities and nursing my own wounds. The level of consensus-building needed to establish a foundation for the changes I encouraged demanded a level of mental agility and fortitude that was unsustainable. I, like many of my comrades in DEAI, acknowledge that feeling safe, valued and protected is fleeting in this work.

We all need to give ourselves permission and encourage each other to recharge. Beyond bringing progressive organizational leaders together and being open to new viewpoints and abilities, the work of DEI requires persistent effort, patience, the resolve to address the biases deeply rooted within us, and a whole lot of self-care and patience.

When I wrote *Inclusion Revolution: The Essential Guide to Dismantling Racial Inequity in the Workplace*, my goal was to spark a fire in readers to take ownership and collectively strengthen our ability to drive tangible change. From my decades in the trenches, I've learned to think of the work of transforming workplaces like a massive, global relay race—millions of us passing the baton, doing a million different things, a million times a day. It's about everyone contributing from where we stand, doing our bit to move this symbolic baton forward.

But I also know that exhaustion is a familiar companion in this DEI work. It often feels like a relentless race toward burnout as we put our all into reshaping systems that are deeply resistant to change. In *Inclusion Revolution*, I encourage readers not to be overwhelmed by this resistance and to lean on each other along the way. But I know that even sidestepping these obstacles can be a Herculean task when our emotional resources are depleted.

We've got to be adept navigators in this tricky terrain, skillfully charting our course to prevent or recover from burnout.

Yes, You: How to Manage DEI When You Don't Think You Know How

Have you ever looked around and wondered, "How on earth did anyone think I'm the right person to lead DEI efforts for my team?"

Here's a secret: DEI practitioners often wonder the same thing, especially when they're feeling beat up and burned out from years of neglect, disrespect, and inability to move the needle, not because of their failed capacities but because of failed systems that limit them in every way, either through minimal budgets, support, or positional influence.

Navigating the intricacies of DEI in the workplace is challenging enough for long-standing practitioners, but it can be even more daunting for managers who don't think of themselves as experts in this space, and yet are responsible for driving progress within their teams and managing the intricate dynamics of DEI in the workplace.

DEI work is multifaceted, with race and gender frequently at the forefront. However, there are other critical dimensions to consider. The "sandwich generation" employees are balancing the care of aging parents and young children. Immigrants often confront xenophobia, not just in broader society but sometimes in the workplace, too. People with disabilities, visible or otherwise, may feel compelled to conceal their identities to blend in. Religious individuals might hesitate to ask for accommodations, such as prayer spaces. Furthermore, employees residing in US states with restrictive reproductive rights laws might have valid concerns regarding their options for family planning. Factor in the complexity of class and generational diversity, and the array of identity dimensions can leave managers in a perpetual state of confusion and stress.

When I joined Vice as chief people officer in May 2020, during the early throes of a pandemic that upended our lives and work, I had no clue that within weeks, we'd be confronted with an internal and global reckoning on racial issues—a challenge for which I found myself uniquely competent to lead the company given my nearly two decades' experience transforming organizational cultures to be more inclusive and equitable.

In those early days on the job, the murder of George Floyd set off a worldwide call for justice and transformation, leaving white managers and executives in a state of paralysis, unsure of how to engage with Black coworkers. The situation's complexity was rooted in a longstanding neglect of these issues. For those of us who had long navigated the professional landscape while contending with discrimination due to our race, gender, or other identities, these challenges were not new.

The reactions across the company were striking. It seemed as though many were just now awakening to the reality of racism. For employees of color, who have long faced these issues, there was an urgent call for solutions and an immediate one.

This left many managers feeling ill-equipped to handle the barrage of reactions, from employees grappling with anger and pain, to anxious clients, apprehensive board members and shareholders, and the looming threat of public scrutiny on social media. The atmosphere was charged as managers across the spectrum grappled with how to respond to and process these significant events.

On a global employee note, I introduced myself to the company and shared resources aimed at helping employees navigate and comprehend racial trauma. My message emphasized our commitment to providing a supportive environment for all employees, particularly BIPOC (Black, Indigenous, and People of Color) employees impacted by compounded health, economic, and racial trauma.

The following week, I sent this note to my team:

My note to Vice global last week was not the introduction I had originally envisioned but it was the message of solidarity and action that I would have wanted to receive from someone in my position. I've received lovely messages of support and encouragement across the globe. One not-so-kind critique that is a natural result of engaging in these difficult conversations. And overall, a sense that we're headed in the right direction when it comes to showing up and showing care for our teams across the globe.

All of this is taking an extraordinary emotional toll on so many of us. Admittedly, I have found it hard to hold space for the grief and outrage I'm feeling.

Like any human, I wasn't immune to the experiences of grief and pain, but the intensity of this moment hit harder. Jacquelyn Ogorchukwu Iyamah, the author of *Racial Wellness*, explains that vicarious racism—the secondary trauma triggered by witnessing, learning about, or educating others regarding racist incidents—can have profound psychological impacts. This kind of exposure can result in depression, anxiety, and stress. It often heightens a state of hypervigilance concerning one's safety and the safety of loved ones and community members. I and many others were carrying that weight. These significant health consequences are detrimental in themselves and can be a direct pathway to burnout.[2]

I wanted to be open about my emotions with my team. This act of vulnerability was pivotal in developing the kind of relationship I aspired to have. Building trust and influence without physical presence was challenging, but I discovered that navigating a crisis together forges a unique sense of community. It also presented a unique opportunity to lead how I would have wanted to be led.

In advising leaders on how to support their teams effectively in coping with the emotional toll and fatigue of DEI in the workplace, I recommend a basic initial approach:

- **Listen:** Actively pay attention to your team members' needs and concerns, as well as any fears or anxieties these might stir up within you.
- **Pause:** Before diving into action, allow yourself a moment to prepare with deep reflection and breathing.
- **Care:** As leadership coach Reggie Butler emphasizes, show "evidence of effort" in handling sensitive matters.[3] Even when the right words are hard to find, expressions like "I'm sorry that you're feeling this right now" or "I'm here whenever you want to talk" can make a significant difference.

This three-step approach can help you navigate complex or uncomfortable moments, whether about DEI outcomes or addressing the unique needs of your teams. Adopting this method can help prevent burnout, benefiting both yourself and those under your leadership.

Addressing Diversity Fatigue

The challenge of diversity fatigue in organizations is intensifying, particularly in an era where commitments to DEI are under attack. This issue is exacerbated as employees, many of whom are dealing with burnout, return to the workplace post-pandemic with changed expectations and an increased demand for equity, inclusion, and a sense of belonging.

Maneuvering through this complex landscape is demanding, particularly for managers committed to offering care and support and implementing positive changes. Organizational change doesn't come from overlooking or denying bias or hostile behaviors; it starts with building a shared understanding of who we are in relation to ourselves and each other.

Throughout my career, I've also grappled with "diversity fatigue." Even in the face of these challenges, I remain committed to these values. Recognizing that this struggle is widespread, I propose the following approach for managers and DEI practitioners looking for effective ways to move forward:

1. **Gain Clarity on What You're Trying to Solve For:** Begin by evaluating the current state of your team: identify the aspects that are working well and those that aren't. Once you've identified the specific areas you want to address, guide your team toward steady progress in three key areas. Reflect on how these efforts will impact you, your team, the broader organization, and potentially the industry. Why three areas? Prioritizing allows you to sideline distractions, secure meaningful metrics, and propel the work forward.

2. **Define the Role You Want to Play:** The goal isn't to endure hardship. You must choose your role to genuinely enable people

from all walks of life to contribute. Whether as an ally, an innovator of new processes and policies, a change advocate, a strategic implementer, a mentor to leaders, or a unifier of allies and advocates, your role can be multifaceted. Embrace a role that resonates with you currently, and remain open to evolving it as your understanding deepens and your organization's needs change.

3. **Take Action:** Develop a concrete plan, implement it, and refine it through testing and iteration. Acknowledge that some missteps are part of the learning curve. Use your resources wisely and galvanize your allies and teams with a clear vision.

A Gentle Reminder

Remember that you're part of a broader community—you are not in this alone. When challenges arise, persist and focus on creating change, one day at a time, one strategy at a time, through setbacks and successes. Building workplaces that work for everyone is a gradual process, and every step counts.

When the Urgency Is Clear But the Roadmap Ahead Is Not, You Build a Way

The reality of DEI work is that it's akin to battling multiple systems with one hand while being pulled down with the other. It's a profoundly challenging sensation, a complex interplay of raw emotions, frustrations, and hope.

When everything around me was spinning in the early phases of the global racial reckoning of 2020, I advocated for a slower, more deliberate pace. I urged managers to adopt a similar stance for themselves and their teams. The times called for reflection, not hasty, grandiose declarations or overambitious pledges.

Facing the immense pressure from every angle—my boss, their colleagues, my peers, and our teams—was daunting. Everyone sought immediate relief through quick-fix solutions: swift statements, rapid actions, and a magic wand to "solve it all now." Amid this whirlwind, I had to dig deep to find the courage to create a space for healing and trust across teams while avoiding premature promises.

To lay the groundwork for progress, we concentrated on building DEI readiness among managers. This meant equipping managers with inclusive leadership skills and a willingness to address organizational inequities. Our goal was to help them build muscles to manage the messy, complex, and human elements of their work. By enhancing their capabilities, we aimed to deepen their impact, thereby better serving the needs of their teams.

Before you wonder—no, we didn't get everything right. There's no magic solution or quick fix for building a culture of inclusion and belonging, but you have to start somewhere. We learned from our missteps and remained steadfast in our commitment to advocating for and incorporating DEI principles into our people and business practices, one step and one mistake at a time.

As someone of Dominican–Puerto Rican descent who has spent a career wading through the complexities of cultural and racial identity within predominantly white corporate spaces, this was also a profoundly liberating moment for me. All the years I had dedicated to developing my skills and tools for maneuvering within these complex spaces finally received the recognition they deserved. In times like these, when the urgency for action is unmistakable but the path forward is less so, I've leaned on my experience and intuition to chart the way ahead. This process involved not only strengthening my abilities but also building the capabilities of others so we could collectively lead the work.

Coping with Racism: Understanding Its Mental Health Impact on Black Communities

In their groundbreaking research, neuroscientists Negar Fani of Emory University and Nathaniel Harnett of Harvard Medical School delve into the effects of racism on brain development and function, focusing mainly on the mental health repercussions for Black communities. Their findings reveal that societal invalidation of racism, along with its pervasive nature and the frequent trivialization or dismissal of its impact, significantly exacerbates its detrimental effects. This leads to profound neurological changes and an increased risk of various diseases.

Arline Geronimus, a public health researcher, coined the term "weathering" to describe the erosion of brain structures resulting from the relentless stress of constant invalidation and the burden of coping with racism. This sustained pressure accelerates biological aging and increases vulnerability to a host of health issues, including burnout, which can lead to premature death in communities of color. To effectively address and mitigate these consequences, it is essential for leaders and managers to actively recognize and challenge their biases toward people of color and marginalized groups. Understanding how these biases can lead to discriminatory behavior and speech is critical in creating healthier, more equitable environments.[4]

Continuing the Work Through Reckonings and Reversals

The racial reckoning of summer 2020 brought long-ignored issues to the forefront, particularly the systemic mistreatment of people of color in workplaces, notably Black employees. Ironically, these same Black workers were then called upon to address racism within their workplaces. This pattern of expecting marginalized groups to solve problems they didn't create is a recurring theme, evident in responses to anti-Asian, anti-Muslim, anti-Jewish, anti-Palestinian, anti-immigrant sentiments, and other forms of prejudice.

Then, in 2023, a backlash long in the making emerged. Several states passed legislation banning DEI programs, and anti-trans legislation spiked, casting a shadow over DEI initiatives. Lawsuits alleging "discriminatory" DEI policies against companies, law firms, government agencies, and nonprofits became a new battlefield. Even the publishing world witnessed ongoing first amendment challenges from book bans to proposed book ratings. The daunting legal challenges left many questioning how to navigate this altered terrain to achieve the long-standing goal of leveling the playing field for women and other marginalized groups.

Throughout my career, I've learned that DEI progress often resembles the tale of Sisyphus: for every setback, there are steps forward, though they might not always be as linear as we'd like. As the dialogue surrounding legal pushbacks continued, I leaned on one aspect: the Supreme Court's decision, despite its implications, still allowed for the ongoing progression and development of DEI initiatives in the workplace.

An unexpected beacon of hope emerged when Nasdaq, an entity not typically associated with pioneering DEI change, became a focal point of optimism. This occurred as an appeals court upheld Nasdaq's mandate requiring diverse board representation. This significant ruling compels publicly traded companies to justify if their boards lack women and minority directors, spotlighting the ongoing push for diversity and inclusion at the highest levels of business leadership. It's a significant step, signaling that we are still moving in the right direction despite the hurdles and distractions.[5]

During times of backlash, I advocate for returning to the beautiful basics rather than retreating. It's an opportunity to assess what is effective and what isn't, and to integrate the successful elements so seamlessly into the very fabric of business operations that their benefits for employees, shareholders, clients, and all stakeholders become undeniable.

In a virtual panel discussion focused on navigating DEI in today's environment, a fellow panelist who is a lawyer observed that the recent backlash against DEI initiatives is prompting companies to adopt more deliberate and impactful approaches. I view this as a positive development. They pointed out that this recent backlash has thrust DEI issues into the spotlight, particularly at the C-suite level, encouraging leaders to assess their DEI initiatives critically. This has led to essential questions such as "Why do we have these programs, and what results are they achieving?" This scrutiny is crucial in ensuring that DEI efforts are not just performative but are effective and result-oriented.

Keeping perspective and differentiating between legal responsibilities and opposition rooted in political motives can be taxing. This is a moment to reevaluate your motivations and motivate yourself and your teams to embrace this work. Here are some ideas for how to do it:

Instead of getting bogged down by distractions or legal concerns, why not concentrate on effectively implementing DEI work? Managers, this is where you can shine. Evaluate your current strategies for their ongoing impact. Do they boost morale, improve retention, and increase employee satisfaction? Are they integral to the well-being and productivity of your teams? When these elements are in place, it becomes much harder to dismantle business-critical programs.

Additionally, empower the DEI leaders with the political capital they often lack. Forge a strong partnership with your DEI teams and learn from them. Supporting and collaborating with them isn't just a matter of ethical leadership; it's also a wise business decision.

As a manager, you have the power to transcend performative actions. It's easy to produce glossy reports, but what matters is the tone set by your CEO, you, and your peers. The true test of DEI effectiveness is whether it's genuinely embedded in the organization versus just a box-ticking exercise. Look beyond the surface. And if there's concern about biases in hiring, such as only reviewing Black candidates—which you shouldn't do—remember, exclusively considering white candidates is equally problematic. It's time for candidness and building the equitable workplaces everyone deserves.

The Glass Cliff: Don't Get Burned (Out)

Seasoned leaders who are women or people of color often confront the reality of the "glass cliff," a term coined by Michelle Ryan and Alex Haslam.[6] In these scenarios, they're more likely to be in executive roles during organizational crises. Rather than leading in stable times, they're handed the reins amid turmoil, tasked with steering through impossible challenges.

This dynamic offers a compelling viewpoint compared to white male leaders' experiences. Ever notice how, when a white male leader fails to uphold ethical standards, they often receive a "golden parachute," providing a soft landing? This situation leaves women and leaders of color to wonder: if the roles were reversed, would the reaction be as lenient or generous? Unfortunately, women and leaders of color rarely enjoy the luxury of second chances in comparable situations. This disparity creates a significant, though frequently unseen, obstacle in the workplace. Their roles, laden with risks and instability, become breeding grounds for burnout, adding another layer to the already complex landscape of leadership diversity.

To mitigate the "glass cliff" risks, organizations must strive for equitable support structures and recognize these leaders' unique challenges. Failure to address this imbalance not only jeopardizes the well-being of individual leaders but also undermines the broader goals of inclusivity and belonging within the workplace.

Inclusion Lessons from an Expert

Global Chief Diversity, Equity, and Inclusion Officer Cindy Pace at MetLife says, "I believe that leaders who want to create inclusive work cultures must start with knowing how to demonstrate inclusion. Inclusion is about consistent, intentional behaviors/actions where people feel truly seen, heard, respected and valued in daily interactions."

She goes on to share three ways to do this: (1) Recognize everyone's contributions, no matter how big or small. (2) Seek and apply diverse perspectives. (3) Give every voice value. No positions, rank, titles, degrees should get in the way of making space for people to speak up even if they disagree.[7]

When We Mess Up

In a *Harvard Business Review* article titled "When Your Efforts to Be Inclusive Misfire," I discussed the importance of addressing issues of inclusivity and injustice, highlighting the potential for unintended harm in well-intentioned efforts.[8] I emphasized that even DEI experts can make mistakes, recounting a personal experience where my attempts to model inclusive allyship inadvertently caused harm and alienation.

I recalled an incident where I sent a company-wide email condemning anti-Semitism and Islamophobia, aiming to promote inclusivity and allyship. However, the email drew the attention of Arab and Palestinian employees in our Middle East offices, who thoughtfully pointed out their concerns with an article linked in the email, which, during a sensitive period in the Palestinian crisis, had muddled the issues of anti-Semitism and Islamophobia. In the article, I write about how my well-intentioned effort for inclusivity had unintentionally led to some employees feeling excluded.

What did I do about it? I managed my emotions and mindset first, then had a long and difficult conversation, ensuring these employees felt listened to and reassured.

Nobody told you this was going to be easy!

This experience underscores the uncomfortable reality that many individuals face in the workplace when navigating conversations about racism, gendered microaggressions, or abusive language. Fear of punishment and rejection often silences employees, including managers, preventing them from speaking up about such issues. However, this silence is a barrier to progress in DEI efforts.

In this era marked by swift demographic changes, rapid technological progress, and shifting social dynamics both inside and beyond the workplace, it is clear that transforming the workplace is an imperative. The insight here is the need to cultivate an environment that welcomes challenging conversations and allows individuals to learn from their mistakes in expressing themselves.

Here's the thing. Engaging in these discussions, even when flawless, is far more beneficial than choosing silence.

Promoting open dialogue, coupled with demonstrating empathy and understanding, is vital. This approach ensures that every current and prospective employee receives equal access and opportunities to enter workplaces, thrive, contribute maximally, and experience a genuine sense of belonging regardless of identity or background.

Employees, this message is also for you: Trust and openness are two-way streets. In numerous organizations, immense effort is being invested to lay the groundwork for your success. However, we can't establish genuinely trusting and productive relationships if your colleagues feel compelled to withhold information or are paralyzed by the fear that you might respond unforgivingly to their errors or, worse, out of apprehension of retribution.

True collaboration flourishes in an environment where open communication and understanding are reciprocal.

Social Issues and Internal Conflicts

Helping employees navigate turbulent times is an important part of every manager's job. However, managers who face increasing pressure to address societal issues, support employee well-being, and maintain a connection to the company's mission and productivity are often uncertain about how to speak and engage with their teams on complex social issues.

Since 2020, there's been a shift in corporate expectations to comment on sociopolitical events, whether directly related to business operations or not. This trend, accelerated by responses to events like George Floyd's murder or the Israel-Hamas conflict, has created an expectation for continuous engagement. Taking a public stand can be risky, but saying nothing might look like you don't care or agree with the wrong side. Your actions must match your words.

In typical fashion, these social issues can turn into internal conflicts that often see one side assigning blame while the other either remains silent or contends that the accusations and "cancel culture" are excessive. Both sides feel unheard, disrespected, and intolerant of the other's viewpoint. This leads to increasingly entrenched positions and contentious debates about who has the right to speak, the boundaries of free speech, and how these concepts fit within corporate culture. Such disputes quickly veer away from the issue at hand, devolving into a meta-argument about the nature of the argument itself. This kind of discourse can become bleak, disheartening, and unproductive for everyone involved. So, setting aside the core complexities, I recommend some principles that have guided me in making decisions about internal and external responses to conflict, recognizing that these guidelines must resonate with internal practices, reinforcing trust among employees and consumers.

Proactive Decision-Making: Build out your response criteria ahead of time to enable swift and empathetic action during crises.

Key Decision-Making Considerations:
- **Alignment with Business, Brand, and Values:** Does the issue align with the company's strategy and core values?
- **Impact on Stakeholders:** Does this issue directly impact employees or local communities? Is there a collective call for a response, action or leadership?
- **Credibility and Potential for Impact:** What is our understanding of the issue? Can we make a meaningful impact, either independently or through collaborations?
- **Assessing the Impact of Action or Inaction:** Will our action make a positive difference or just add another voice? What are the effects of over- or under-engagement? Is a public statement or pledge sufficient, or are more substantial actions required?

Cultivating a Supportive Environment:
- **Embrace Mistakes and Learning:** Mistakes will happen. Creating a safe space for employee expression, knowing that misunderstandings and hurt feelings will arise, and learning from these errors is essential.
- **Support in Emotional Moments:** Recognize the fear, confusion, and desire to be heard and understood among team members with diverse opinions and experiences.
- **Set Healthy Boundaries:** While providing support, remember to care for your well-being—your resources are limited, and self-care is essential, so don't forget to lean on others for support.

- **Addressing Burnout:** Stay alert to burnout symptoms in yourself and your team. This can manifest as defensiveness, irritability, physical symptoms, or low energy. Maintaining perspective during challenging times is crucial.

The world is messy and it will continue to test our empathy, grace, and knowledge. In my experience, organizations with established systems and processes can compassionately and diligently guide their workforce during difficult moments. While we may stumble in our efforts, inaction isn't the solution. We can start by trying to deepen our understanding and compassion.

In *Breaking Through: Communicating to Open Minds, Move Hearts, and Change the World,*[9] Sally Sussman offers a decision-making framework:

- How does it relate to our purpose? Our purpose is breakthroughs that change patients' lives. We have a wide berth on issues relating to healthcare. But we shouldn't get involved in every issue, because you lose your agency if you speak on every issue.
- How does it impact our most important stakeholders? For us, that's patient groups and our employees, but every entity has its own set of special stakeholders.
- How does it relate to our values? At Pfizer, we have four values. Courage, excellence, equity, and joy. And I'm not saying, how does it relate to our politics? Because there's no place in my mind for politics in business, but there's plenty of room for values.
- What are our options here? Because sometimes, companies and institutions can be very reactive. They feel pressed because a journalist is calling, or they feel pressed because somebody wants them to sign a petition by a deadline. I try to reject that kind of false pressure, step back, form more ideas in our words carefully, and then come out when we're ready. Because the worst thing you can do in these circumstances is to ping pong. You've really got to be sure.
- What is the price of our silence? Because I believe that there are some issues, violence in the school, racism, where the silence is deafening. And as good corporate citizens, you need to speak out.

The Uneven Workplace Journeys

Navigating the corporate landscape as a woman of color can often resemble the delicate art of juggling flaming swords. It's a challenging feat that can often result in feelings of isolation and exposure to unforgiving scrutiny.

"That was an excellent presentation, but your outfit lacked professionalism," commented a white senior female executive to a Latina mid-level manager who had just delivered a report on their Latino employee resource group's progress to the executive team. She added, "It's distracting." The manager, dressed in a printed dress shirt with tasteful accessories, couldn't help but wonder: What about this attire was deemed unprofessional or distracting? After all, this is what I wear to church!

Racially insensitive comments are unquestionably hurtful, and biased remarks can seep into and adversely affect one's career progression. While the Latina manager had every reason to be upset, as did I when I heard this story along with two members of the company's diversity leadership during dinner, I was deeply impressed by how she maintained her composure even in such a heated moment. When we inquired about her response, she shared, "I was caught off guard and simply said thank you. However, I will choose the right moment to convey how that comment made me feel."

This was an ill-considered, prejudiced comment—a carelessness we should all endeavor to steer clear of.

Fostering trusting relationships can become significantly more challenging when one is continually subjected to casual devaluation and offhand racist remarks. Have you ever wondered whether your attire unintentionally perpetuates stereotypes about Latinx individuals? I certainly have. Perhaps you've questioned, "Does this bold red lipstick and vibrant floral dress make me appear as though I'm auditioning for a telenovela?" Or maybe you've hesitated to wear those hoops at a company function, concerned that they might evoke images of Jennifer Lopez or some other Latina stereotype in the minds of your colleagues. Regardless, if you're asked to speak, your voice deserves recognition, regardless of your style or background.

Such comments often stem from individuals grappling with their biases and clinging to antiquated notions of professionalism. For far too long, those aspiring to be viewed as possessing executive presence and leadership potential have felt compelled to adopt the persona of a middle-aged, cisgender, straight, white man to be taken seriously. These outdated perceptions continue to perpetuate a lack of diversity at the highest echelons of organizations.

To garner respect and build a following, it should be about embracing your authentic self without feeling coerced into donning someone else's ill-fitting attire.

Being authentic is easy when you're surrounded by people who look like you. But showing up as your true self can be daunting if you represent anything resembling any difference from traditional leadership markers.

Well-educated, well-intentioned, and even open-minded individuals often underestimate the impact of privilege and access, allowing some to navigate workplaces easily while others encounter countless barriers. This inequality manifests in the professional lives of women, people of color, LGBTQ individuals, and other marginalized groups.

Throughout my career, I've had to tread carefully, balancing being true to myself and not crossing any invisible boundaries. I monitored my tone, adjusted my hairstyle, and opted for conservative clothing and accessories to evade being typecast into the "sexy and loud Latina" stereotype.

While the men around me boldly occupied spaces and celebrated their accomplishments, I kept my achievements understated, shunning any hint of seeking undue attention. Why? It was all about conforming to a "corporate" image and assimilating to achieve success.

As Adam Grant pointed out in a social media post on September 17, 2023, authenticity isn't about expressing every opinion you hold; it's about ensuring that your voice reflects your values.[10] But expressing these values can be challenging when your presence is difficult for others to accept.

We've encouraged individuals to bring their authentic selves to the workplace for years. Yet we must reflect on how we feel about that authenticity and accommodate it in our meeting rooms, hallways, and virtual spaces.

As a woman of color, I've encountered moments and comments that have offended or hurt me, and regrettably, I've also unintentionally offended others. When faced with workplace disagreements or misunderstandings, I've learned to collect my thoughts and emotions before addressing the issue with my coworkers. I respond assertively, using "I" statements, and I often inject humor or kindness to defuse the tension. For instance, I might say, "When you restated my recommendation in the recap meeting without giving me credit, I felt erased from our conversation. I value our work relationship. Can you help me understand why my contribution was omitted?" Alternatively, I might playfully remark, "When you confused me for the other Latina on the floor, I felt like we were both invisible to you. And I think I'm pretty memorable!"

To clarify, the responsibility for fostering healthy interactions should not fall on women, people of color, or members of marginalized communities. To proactively build more meaningful relationships, consider the following questions:

- How can I focus on the content of what the person is saying, rather than solely on their delivery or appearance?
- What additional information do I need to truly comprehend my colleague's message, rather than dismissing or avoiding it?
- Before addressing an uncomfortable comment from someone, ask yourself whether you're responding because you feel shut down, ignored, or offended, or if you're seeking to be right.

When both parties are willing, there are constructive ways to respond that can lead to productive conversations and mutual understanding.

In the early part of my career, as the only Latina and the youngest person in most rooms, I often fell prey to what Kenyi Yoshino has coined "covering," the practice of downplaying who you are to survive in an organizational context.[11] I was just learning to find my voice while also learning a new corporate language. I had to build navigational tools for a corporate culture that was very white—white in terms of representation and white in terms of unwritten rules of professional conduct. I had no safety net nor a compass to tell me which direction I should face. I was lucky to find allies who saw me, supported me, and challenged me. That's not the experience for many women, people of color, and other marginalized employees.

You simply can't perform at your best when you're constantly modifying or playing down who you are, including your appearance, your body language, your accents, your abilities, your communication style, and who you love.[12]

Wake-Up Call from 2023: A decade has passed since Professor Yoshino's and Deloitte's pivotal study "Uncovering Talent" first made waves.[13] Fast forward to today, and his latest findings are a stark reminder. A staggering 60% of US workers have been covering at work in the last year.[14] The trend is even more pronounced among those with marginalized identities. The more aspects of their identity they feel pressured to conceal, the more they engage in covering at work.

Women, people of color, individuals with disabilities, and other marginalized workers are flat-out exhausted. They're beaten down from pressures to downplay aspects of their identity. They're tired of having to constantly break down their lived experiences so that others can understand. They are exhausted from being the ones responsible for diffusing passive (and sometimes not-so-passive) racism and fed up with building their own safety nets. Weary of navigating their days while being misgendered, confused for someone else, called by the wrong name or pronoun, or judged based on their identities. And let's not forget the sheer fatigue of being asked to provide solutions (often without compensation) to fix workplace culture problems that they didn't create.

As a manager, your mission is to effectively address this persistent workplace issue. Your goal? To create an environment that not only supports but celebrates authenticity. Strive to build a space where each team member feels free to be themselves without hiding or blending in. This approach can boost individual well-being and foster a culture of openness and acceptance.

What Gets in the Way

I'm frequently asked about what gets in the way of DEI progress. Here's what I say:

- Diversity fatigue is real. Despite slow and hard-earned progress, endless battles, discussions, and emotional labor breed frustration and exhaustion, leading to passivity and disengagement.
- DEI is a multifaceted battle. The complexity of DEI and the fear of making mistakes against a daunting array of issues, from sexism to ageism, can be overwhelming. This is often compounded by internal disagreements and the paralysis of not knowing where to start, leading to inaction.

(continued)

(*continued*)

- Addressing the wrong problems. In DEI efforts, there's a tendency to focus on representation while overlooking root causes. The emphasis often lies on recruiting underrepresented individuals but not sufficiently on their success once they join.
- Lack of a shared understanding of what DEI means. The average white male manager is often thinking, "I'm a white man, and I feel like I can't do anything right. I'm on the wrong side of diversity." But there's only one side where everyone feels included and that they belong. This misconception underscores the need for a collective, inclusive approach to DEI, involving everyone's participation.[15]

Seeking to Understand Others Begins with Understanding Ourselves

The conversations that demand the most courage, the ones that hold the most potential to foster a deeper understanding and drive meaningful change, are often the ones we have with ourselves.

I've personally witnessed how managers can drive change within workplaces, not merely by relying on standard management techniques but by adopting an inclusive and equitable mindset that guides their decision-making.

When you're uncertain about how to lead DEI efforts in your organization, remember this: When managers model inclusive behaviors, it sends a compelling message throughout teams and organizations. It normalizes and lends credibility to behaviors that promote trust, well-being, motivation, collaboration, and a sense of belonging. All of which lead to better performance.

By treating your teams with respect, compassion, and inclusivity and providing fair treatment and opportunities, you level the playing field and underscore how crucial diversity, inclusion, and equity for all truly are. By treating yourself with respect and compassion, you model the way for others.

So how can managers who are navigating a messy and often exhausting landscape, sometimes leaving their industries at twice the rate of individual contributors, effectively lead inclusively and with an equitable lens?

Start by reflecting on some critical questions:

- What aspects of this work energize and intimidate me?
- From which industries, fields, or experts can I draw knowledge?
- How would I implement DEI initiatives differently?
- Whose narratives and perspectives am I including, and which ones am I overlooking?
- Perhaps most crucially, am I, or are we collectively, contributing to the obstacles faced by members of my team?

Embrace your courage, especially when you realize your teams and colleagues rely on your professional and emotional support. They may enter work environments where they may not feel seen, valued, or believed. You can change that.

The Universal Desire to Be Heard, Seen, and Valued Is Not Universally Experienced

It's quite possible for people to be hired at top companies, be invited to meetings, and even be asked to speak up and contribute, and still not feel that people like them belong there. We all want to be where we feel competent, supported, and encouraged to grow, and where we feel a deep connection to our work and peers.

Indeed, like any other endeavor, DEI isn't about perfection; it's about progress. It's about asking the tough questions, acknowledging past mistakes, and committing to continuous growth. It's about amplifying underrepresented voices, dismantling systemic barriers, and ensuring everyone has an equal seat at the table.

Yes, there will be discomfort and uncertainty. But that's precisely why this work is so crucial. Through these challenges, we learn, grow, and evolve as individuals and as a society.

The pursuit of DEI isn't just a goal—it's a shared responsibility, a business necessity, and a moral imperative. It's a key element of this grand experiment we call working together.

Creating workplaces that are fair, collaborative, and equitable, where everyone feels they belong, takes sustained effort and hard work. And it takes all of us. It also requires us to be good partners to each other and to the business, because we need each other on this journey. A fundamental expectation is that we show care, trust, and respect to each other, each and every day. That means also operating with integrity and consistency. And that when we mess up—because we are human—that we admit it, get back up, and do better.

Recognizing the warning signs of burnout is not just about supporting ourselves and each other; it's an act of self-preservation and empowerment. We uphold our resilience and perseverance by proactively caring for our mental and emotional well-being. This self-care is essential, as it fuels our capacity to continue the challenging yet rewarding journey toward creating inclusive workplaces. Remember, prioritizing our own health is a powerful form of self-leadership, crucial for sustaining the long-term impact of DEI.

Let the Sparks Fly: How We Grow

Navigating the complexities of DEI in the workplace requires continuous effort, empathy, and a collective effort to build a shared understanding of who we are in relation to ourselves and each other. Managers and DEI practitioners often contend with substantial emotional labor, balancing high expectations and, often, backlash. To ease this burden, it's essential for managers to actively listen, value their team's diverse voices and needs, learn from mistakes, and maintain perseverance. Addressing diversity fatigue through self-awareness, self-care, and support for those leading this work is vital for sustaining resilience and preventing burnout. Let's now turn our attention to scripts that can help you reignite your DEI spark.

Scripts for Managers and DEIB Practitioners

Managers:

- "As we face these DEI challenges, let's prioritize open dialogue and understanding. Your voice is heard and integral to our collective progress in DEI. It's crucial to acknowledge our mistakes and learn from them. Remember, we're in this together."
- "Team, as we navigate our DEI journey, I want us to take a moment to reflect. Reflect on our actions, experiences, biases, fears, expectations, and roles in this effort. It's not always easy, and it requires courage to confront the uncomfortable truths about ourselves and our workplace. But it's necessary. Our goal is to support each other in meaningful ways to build a team where everyone feels valued, heard,

and understood. Let's be courageous together, not just in our words, but in our actions."

- "Team, I want to remind everyone that our commitment to DEI is not a one-time initiative; it's a continuous and shared journey. This journey involves learning, growing, and sometimes facing discomfort and uncertainty. These challenges are part of our evolution as individuals and as a team. Let's embrace this work with an open mind and heart, recognizing that the path to a truly inclusive and equitable workplace is ongoing."

DEIB Practitioners:

- "Let's focus on three areas that need improvement and work collaboratively towards these goals, recognizing that change doesn't happen overnight, but through consistent effort and dedication."
- "While we've made progress, not everyone may feel a sense of belonging or feel that they can thrive in this workplace. Let's avoid assuming that our current efforts suffice and instead delve deeper. By actively seeking feedback, listening empathetically, and making necessary adjustments, we can ensure that all team members feel valued and supported."
- "As DEI practitioners, we are on a never-ending journey of growth and learning. This path is filled with challenges and discomfort, but it's essential for our personal and collective evolution. Let's embrace these challenges as opportunities to learn and grow and allow ourselves space and distance when we need to rest and replenish."

6

Find Awe at Work: How to Turn Your Work Nightmares into Epic Adventures

"Where do I begin?" I wondered, as I closed my eyes.

I was in a review meeting with an executive coach supporting one of our senior leaders. I was expecting the conversation to be about the leader, and was caught off-guard by his sudden, introspective question: "What's your top worry at work right now?"

The truth was that most days, I felt like I was playing a rapid round of Tetris with blocks falling from the sky—escalating financial and market pressures, global social tensions, everyday people problems, and the lingering work-life aftershocks of a pandemic. Each day presented a new challenge in fitting together these unpredictable pieces, and the game seemed set to expert mode.

But one worry soon overshadowed the rest: "The growing anger and frustration among our managers deeply troubles me," I told him.

I went on, "It's like a dark, pervasive shadow hanging over their daily interactions, a breeding ground for workplace nightmares." Chronic fear driven from uncertainty about the state of the world and crippling resource constraints not only slowed down creativity and productivity but, more significantly, wore down managers and their teams. Beyond communication breakdowns, it showed up in the bitterness and snarkiness of their interactions. This realization hit me hard: the widespread dissatisfaction and exhaustion that led to destructive behaviors and eroded trust also stifled the potential for joy and awe in our professional lives.

And it was a ticking bomb for widespread burnout.

I observed managers crumbling under the pressures of crushing workloads and social tensions, often resorting to knee-jerk reactions and venting rather than taking a moment to reflect. Who had the time for pause, anyway? The superficial issues, like disrespect and impatience toward team members, were indicators of more profound, systemic problems. These behaviors created a nightmarish environment.

For instance, I once confronted a manager about their disrespectful behavior toward junior team members and he said, "This is ridiculous. They're all useless. If it weren't for me, this place would go down." Sigh. This case of problematic behavior was going to be a tough one. His reaction, combining a sense of hubris, isolation, and struggle beneath a tough exterior, was all too familiar and heart-wrenching.

Stepping into the role of a reflective mirror, I asked, "Let's assume everything you're saying is true. What does that say about you?"

This question is designed to stop us in our tracks—it's uncomfortable but necessary for a shift in perspective. Over time, and through many such dialogues, we started to make headway. That particular manager began earnestly exploring and understanding their role in exacerbating their team's and their own work conditions. It was a slow, nonlinear process of self-discovery and change, one tough conversation at a time.

Because here's the thing: At the heart of workplace nightmares is extreme stress, which can push workers toward burnout and fuel negative emotional responses. This stress leads to a fragile sense of self, making concepts like accountability, trust, and loyalty feel out of reach. At the same time, the often necessary, relentless pursuit of efficiency and cost-cutting can cast a long shadow over the essential elements of nurturing a balanced workplace. And to top it all off, deep-rooted cultural issues such as gender biases and racism add to an already daunting and disheartening atmosphere, further increasing the risk of burnout.

In other words, we have our work cut out for us!

But there's hope. The very operational inefficiencies and interpersonal tensions that cause so much anxiety and distrust are the pathway to finding awe at work. By proactively tackling these issues head-on, even before they morph into full-blown nightmares, we can transform our workplaces into spaces brimming with joy and inspiration. The key lies in fostering a culture steeped in self-awareness compassion and courage.

In this chapter, I want to reengage you with the elements of your work that first sparked your enthusiasm and passion. It's about revisiting and realigning with our fundamental values, those core principles that initially set us on our professional paths. I will share strategies and insights on transforming the shadow of burnout into a renewed light of engagement and reignited sense of awe in our professional lives, helping us to see our work not just as a series of tasks but as a purposeful journey filled with opportunities for growth, fulfillment, and rediscovery of joy.

Embrace a Beginner's Mindset

Do you remember the rush of excitement when you landed your first job or were last promoted? Those initial days brimmed with potential, and everything seemed achievable. The thrill of new relationships, projects, and opportunities lifted you from the ground.

Do you also remember when that initial spark fizzled out? When situations that were once exciting began to feel stale? It might have started when someone quit, and you had to take on their workload with no change in salary or deadlines, spiraling into exhaustion, breeding loneliness and frustration. Gradually, you might have felt like you couldn't do anything right, and you became disenchanted with your boss and/or colleagues.

You were burned out.

And it's not just you who feels the impact of going from a bright-eyed beginner to a weary, overburdened drudge. Your colleagues, the people you manage, your family and friends, they all sense it too. You might find yourself contemplating a job change, or you've already slipped into "quiet quitting" mode, trudging through each day. This scenario often indicates it's time for reflection and change.

You know you need a new beginning. But what exactly is a beginner's mind?

In the classic Zen text *Zen Mind, Beginner's Mind*, Shunryu Suzuki writes, "In the beginner's mind there are many possibilities, but in the expert's mind there are few."[1] Embracing a "beginner's mind," or *Shoshin* from Zen Buddhism, means approaching the world with the openness and curiosity of a novice. This mindset, free from past knowledge and biases, expands our perspective and potential, and can help us break free from feeling stuck or burnt out. It's about retaining a sense of wonder, eagerness to learn, curiosity, and openness to new methods.

While this approach doesn't discard the expertise that brought you status, prominent roles, and success, it enriches it by remaining adaptable and exploratory, rekindling the excitement and awe of initial discovery. What if we could recapture that sense of excitement, curiosity, and energy when you first learned something new? That sense of awe is still within you and can be rekindled, benefiting you and those around you.

Here are a few tips, inspired by executive coaching and Buddhist principles, to cultivate your beginner's mind:

- **Get Curious:** Shake off that autopilot mode and encourage your mind to imagine and wonder. Be open to trying new things and learning from mistakes. Channel your inner five-year-old's relentless curiosity—you know, the one who incessantly asks, "What's this?" and "How does this thingamajig work?" Slowing down to feed your curiosity can lead you to smarter solutions that might have zoomed past you at your usual, impatient speed. Dive into conversations with a "tell me more" attitude, and watch as you build more profound, meaningful connections. Who knew channeling your inner Curious George could be such a game-changer?

- **Observe Before Reacting:** Never underestimate your potential to achieve great things during life's quieter moments. Meditation has taught me a valuable lesson—to observe the "monkeys" in my mind, those racing thoughts and sensations, without immediately passing judgment. This practice is useful in everyday interactions. When someone's comments irk you, pause and think about the reason behind your irritation instead of instantly reacting. Watch these feelings with an open mind without rushing to conclusions. Giving yourself the space to process and respond thoughtfully rather than reactively can transform your reactions and enhance your understanding of yourself and others.

- **Watch Your Self-Talk:** When did you last say, "Good job!" "You are worthy," or "It's OK" to yourself? Ease up on the self-roasting and throw yourself a little party now and then. Challenge the narratives you've carried since childhood about your limitations, fears of betrayal, or need for control. When others disappoint you, consider their humanity and struggles. There's a profound sense of freedom in loosening the grip on rigidly held beliefs or situations that previously unsettled you. Letting go of past-based assumptions allows you to see conditions for what they are and to offer others (and yourself) grace.

By practicing these steps, you can reignite the enthusiasm and openness of a beginner's mind, helping you turn workplace nightmares into moments of growth and grace for yourself and your teams.

Find Your Harmony in the Hamster Wheel

Have you ever felt like you're on a hamster wheel at work, trapped in an endless loop of tasks that leave you drained and wondering if you're making any real difference? Welcome to the "Hamster Wheel Effect," where work cycles into repetitive, often unproductive tasks that can lead to burnout, especially when leading others. The real challenge is to remind ourselves of what we love about our work as we determine whether our efforts are effective or just spinning wheels, particularly in areas we can't control.

Think about those high-pressure periods—end-of-quarter rushes, looming deadlines, or high-stakes project launches. I vividly recall the toll of juggling multiple enterprise-wide projects amid a relentless cycle of shifting priorities and a backlog of unfinished tasks throughout the pandemic. The directive to "Drop everything for today's priority," only to pivot weeks later, often left me and my team reeling from confusion, frustration, and exhaustion. It was debilitating for us all.

While prevalent in many workplaces, this cycle deeply affected our efficiency and mental well-being. More than just stressful, these relentless crunch periods risk burnout, depression, and health issues, undermining trust and self-esteem and compromising the stability and focus crucial in a work environment. Reflecting on these experiences, it's clear that finding sustainable ways to manage such pressures is essential for maintaining both professional productivity and personal well-being.

In the past, I've walked away from enviable jobs to reset boundaries and regain control over my work-life balance, plagued by relentless workplace nightmares. I've since realized that quitting in response to an awful boss or impossible demands isn't the only escape from burnout. Sometimes the overlooked solution is achieving balance and harmony in our current roles, hamster wheels and all. Here's what has been effective for me when resigning wasn't an option or the right choice:

- **Reignite Your Passion and Purpose at Work:** Take a mental note of whatever work activities invigorate you, then actively seek to incorporate more of that into your routine. Where do you want to grow in leading people? What about your work do you want to outlive you? I've recaptured my spark when mentoring junior team members. Transforming what could be routine supervisory meetings into sessions of meaningful engagement and growth has not only been fulfilling for me but also empowering for those I mentor. This brings new life into my day-to-day work life, reminding me why I love what I do and the purpose of my role.
- **Collect Moments of Joy:** On those challenging days when work feels overwhelming, I find solace in my "Happy Folder." It's a collection of positive messages and affirming reminders of my impact. These notes—from junior employees, colleagues, and even external partners—are a tangible reminder that the work I do matters and that even the smallest of gestures can leave a lasting, positive imprint. For instance, I treasure a farewell note from one of my team members that concluded with these words: "I appreciate everything you've done for me. I know you advocate for us even though we may not see it sometimes, but we sense it." This simple yet effective practice helps recenter my focus and boosts my morale, reaffirming the value of my contributions.
- **Find Humor in the Hamster Wheel:** Stuck in a cycle of neverending meetings? Wrestling with vague project expectations? Seek your balance with a dash of humor and a smile, your secret weapons in navigating and acknowledging the workplace absurdities we all face. When assessing the necessity of my presence in meetings, I ask

with a smile, "Do you need me, or is there someone better suited for this? Perhaps there's a chance for someone else to shine?" This approach helps in setting boundaries and maintaining sanity amid the chaos. Sometimes a shared chuckle over the zaniness of work is the best way to build solidarity and keep your sanity intact.

- **Pause and Reflect:** When you find yourself facing roadblocks on your expressway to Burnoutville, it's a good time to hit the brakes and think about these questions:
  - What feelings is this situation bringing up for me?
  - What would my future, wiser self do to change this situation?
  - What is fixed, and what is flexible in this scenario?
  - If I were a superhero, what superpower would I use right now?

A slight shift in perspective or approach can change everything. Studies show that employees who can harmonize their professional and personal lives report higher job and life satisfaction, along with reduced depression and anxiety.[2,3] By taking these steps, you regain control over your work life and inspire others to find their rhythm in the chaos. Leading by example, you can show that navigating work demands with intention, balance, and lightness is possible.

What Lights You Up?

Several months into the pandemic, I found myself engulfed in melancholy. Every day I solved problems for colleagues I'd never physically met and planned strategies for returning to offices I had never been in. Deprived of oxytocin from missing direct interactions, vital for building attachment and trust, I felt the strain of disconnection among our employees.[4] This, combined with a pervasive uncertainty, disconnection and fear, made it challenging to find inspiration.

However, this shifted one afternoon during a marketing campaign presentation showcasing our editorial projects and films. Watching the creative brilliance of teams worldwide, I was struck by the vibrant talent across our organization. It wasn't just another virtual meeting observing creative concepts and snazzy taglines. It was about seeing the joy and pride on my colleagues' faces, feeling their spirits lift with each accolade. In that instant, my focus shifted from personal sadness and an endless to-do list to joyful moments of shared humanity, creativity, and resilience.

How often do you take a moment to appreciate what makes your work special? Inspiring and meaningful work isn't just about your job title or where your desk is. It's about making a positive impact, finding joy in what you do with others, and adding a touch of magic to your daily grind. Discovering what lights us up allows us to counteract burnout from the world's demands, replacing it with grace, kindness, and fulfillment.

In other words, remember that work is not all about ticking boxes; it's about collaborating with others to make and build things that we couldn't do alone and positively impact those around us.

Sure, teaming up with people who are different from you can bring its own set of challenges. Taking the initiative to tackle small issues early can make a difference. Working through these challenges as a team can strengthen your collective bond and create opportunities for shared moments of laughter and camaraderie.

So I invite you to ask yourself: What aspects of my work bring me joy? How can I positively influence my team? How can I spread good vibes for others and create a ripple effect? Reflecting on these questions can help you focus on what truly matters to you and bring a sense of fulfillment and magic to your team's work environment.

At its best, work is about service and collaborative creations with others.

When craving that oxytocin boost, consider joining meetings and presentations that reconnect you with why you do what you do at your organization. I've found that this approach can transform work into a space of lightness, countering the world's harshness and reigniting our connection, motivation, and collective spark.

Don't Expect Authenticity Without Reciprocity

The mantra of "bringing your authentic self to work" often clashes with the willingness of people to accept their colleagues in their full human complexity. Anna Sutton's research at the University of Waikato pinpoints a crucial link between authenticity and well-being in both personal and professional life, showing that authentic self-expression leads to stronger relationships and less conflict, particularly in Western cultures.[5]

In my team-leading adventures, I've discovered the value of reciprocity and honesty, including confessing to my not-so-stellar moments. Ditching the "flawless leader" façade, embracing my imperfections, bad jokes and mistakes, and accepting the same in others. This authenticity slices through rigid work expectations, setting the stage for a more chilled-out, happier me and team.

Imagine the ripple effect of such openness to authenticity in nightmarish work scenarios like dealing with an underperforming team member or a micromanaging leader. When team members aren't pressured to conceal aspects of their identity, like their sexual orientation or disabilities, or feel the need to modify their appearance or accent to blend in, it cultivates an environment where everyone truly belongs. And when those inevitable work challenges crop up, a team grounded in authenticity and trust is better equipped to overcome them without succumbing to burnout.

Embrace a Community Abundance Mindset

"When we help ourselves,
We find moments of happiness.
When we help others,
We find lasting fulfillment."[6]

—Simon Sinek

In a conversation with Shannon Cassidy, host of the *R. O. G (Return on Gratitude)* podcast,[7] I shared that my leadership style is rooted in the joy of building a sense of community, which goes beyond just managing teams. It's about cultivating a space where ideas are nurtured, support and mentorship thrive, and collaboration is sparked. This aspect of my leadership brings me immense happiness and purpose, especially when dealing with work nightmares.

As a Latina, I find deep meaning in community, rooted in generosity, respect, and humility. Everyone who meets my family becomes part of our extended family, our community. That's why building genuine relationships has been a labor of love, not a job, particularly in environments that often overlook authentic connections. Nurturing relationships demands effort but feels like nurturing a giving tree, not a draining life force. It involves:

1. **Leading with Generosity:** I approach relationships with a giving mindset. In her book, *The Lost Art of Connecting,*[8] Susan McPherson emphasizes the importance of approaching relationships with the question "How can I be of assistance?" rather than expecting something in return. Make the introductions that will expand your community's networks and resources, celebrate their achievements, and amplify their work.
2. **Showing Up, Always:** True support means showing up for others at the events that matter to them, celebrating their successes like a book launch, or standing by them in challenging times, like supporting them through a job loss.
3. **Check In, Consistently:** Regular check-ins offering to lend a hand on a project, sharing resources, or sending "thinking of you" messages can strengthen bonds.

These principles form my approach to professional relationships into a network of mutual support and growth that is so necessary when work nightmares make you feel extra crispy.

From Bad Meetings to Treasured Gatherings

Picture this: A punctual meeting where the designated leader outlines the agenda and expected outcomes, and provides relevant materials. The meeting leader also takes a moment for self-reflection on how to improve results and ensures that all participants leave with a clear understanding of the following actions and their responsibilities.

Sounds like the work of a seasoned professional, right? Actually, this is how my teenage daughter has conducted her student-parent-teacher conferences since middle school!

Admittedly, I don't always manage my meetings with the same level of expertise. Comparing my daughter's effective leadership in school meetings to poorly run work meetings is pretty striking. Her ability to facilitate discussions, reflect on progress, and address areas for improvement with the support of her teacher contrasts starkly with many corporate meetings. Poor management often leads to issues like avoidance of responsibility and confusion in typical work meetings, resulting in wasted time, disengagement, and interpersonal tensions. Even companies experimenting with "mandatory meeting-free days" struggle with persistently bad meetings that drain collaboration and enthusiasm.[9]

Good leadership must extend to meetings, and adopting a stewardship mindset could be the solution. Imagine if all work meetings were led with a deliberate focus on the attendees' relevance, clear objectives, and fearless discussions about what really gets in the way, including poor decision-making, power battles, and resource constraints.

In other words, imagine if meetings were of service.

Steven G. Rogelberg from the University of North Carolina Charlotte provides insightful perspectives on stewardship in the context of meetings.[10]

1. **Mindset:** Embrace the role of a time and energy steward for your team and peers, making deliberate meeting decisions from start to finish.

2. **Set Up for Success:** Avoid over-inviting, set shorter meeting times, and structure agenda items as questions to be answered for clarity and efficiency.

3. **Use Video:** Combat social loafing, the human tendency to reduce effort and motivation when working in a group, using video that helps reduce anonymity and enhances engagement. Note: For this to work, everyone must show their image, not hide behind a dark box.

4. **Managing Productivity:** Start and end on time, set norms on everything from when to take breaks to how to treat each other, actively facilitate to draw in all voices and interrupt unhelpful dialogue, and use engagement and interactive polling tools like Slido, Poll Everywhere, or Zoom polls to enhance participation.

5. **End Effectively:** Clearly define takeaways, action steps, and responsible individuals.

6. **Gather Feedback:** Seek input to improve future meetings. Don't be afraid to ask what worked and what didn't.

While perfection is unrealistic, intentional decisions and a stewardship approach can result in efficient and, I dare say, meaningful meetings.

Here's how I approached it: In my biweekly meetings with direct reports, I proactively sent out agendas, solicited time-sensitive topics, and encouraged open dialogue and relationship building. To make sure our meetings were not just transactional but also opportunities for reconnection and exploring personal aspects we might have overlooked, we started with a prompt question shared in advance, like:

- When did you feel most alive and most drained this week?
- What do you want work to be about for you?
- What are you creating or transforming through your work?
- How do you channel joy, hope, and optimism?
- Where do you want to travel next?

Have you ever cringed at the word "icebreaker"? I've been there but have come to appreciate the joy of finding the perfect icebreaker for a meeting. During an advisory board meeting for C-Suite Coach, a consultancy focused on workplace equity and inclusion, founder Angelina Darrisaw asked a brilliant icebreaker question: "Most people in business have that 'Look, Mama, I made it moment.' What was yours?"[11] Laughter ensued, and we felt a warm connection. Questions like "What motivates you?" and "What's the riskiest thing you've done since you turned the corner in a decade (age 30, 40, 50, 60, etc.)?" and "What are you working on to become a better person?" can foster meaningful conversations in professional and personal development settings, encouraging introspection and open communication. They are valuable tools for improving understanding, teamwork, and personal growth. Let's welcome them as opportunities to uncover treasures among us.

Applying these techniques can reshape business interactions and relationships, turning dull, unproductive meetings into opportunities for genuine connection and personal growth. This shift not only makes the time spent in meetings worthwhile but also helps prevent common workplace frustrations.

Unspoken Pain: Understanding Workplace Trauma and Burnout

While burnout can occur without trauma, prior experiences with trauma can lead to burnout. Trauma can increase vulnerability to stress and reduce resilience, making individuals more susceptible to burnout. Emotional exhaustion from hypervigilance, mistrust, and lack of connections at work—an essential aspect of burnout—is often heightened in trauma survivors.

But what about workplace trauma?

In the often-silent world of workplace trauma, countless individuals navigate professional life burdened by an invisible weight. This silent specter is particularly prevalent among women of color, who face additional scrutiny and judgment. Why do we remain silent? The reasons are complex: conditioned norms of "professionalism," fear of judgment, and the ongoing healing journey.

Emotional struggles are often dismissed in the workplace, yet a storm of emotions rages beneath the surface. Stereotypes and biases introduce an extra layer of complexity, especially for those who have long contended with being labeled a "diversity hire," challenging misconceptions about their achievements and combating the false notion that they haven't earned their position.

Acknowledging this burden is the first step toward mitigating burnout. By recognizing each person's talent and unique experiences, we can begin to dismantle these stereotypes and redefine success.

Healing from workplace trauma is a personal journey. It involves understanding the impact of toxic environments, bullying bosses, and discrimination. The process of healing is about more than acknowledging pain; it's about extending compassion and recognizing resilience and growth potential.

Organizations can combat burnout by fostering a trauma-informed workplace culture. In "The Relationship Between Trauma and Burnout," HR consultant Stephanie Lamek recommends the following practices:

- Empower employees to have control and autonomy.
- Ensure role clarity to avoid conflict and ambiguity.
- Foster a collaborative environment.[12]

(continued)

(continued)

Recognizing and supporting employees, offering growth opportunities, and ensuring work-life balance are crucial. Managers should implement trauma-informed principles like empowerment and collaboration to prevent burnout and improve workplace well-being. This approach involves creating open conversation spaces and extending compassion to ourselves and others. Through such practices, healing can begin incrementally, highlighting that our resilience is a defining strength beyond our experiences of trauma.

Managing Conflict in the Workplace

Have you ever witnessed workplace chatter escalate into epic showdowns? At the start of the 2023 Israel-Hamas war, ordinary team meetings could feel like gladiatorial battles, filled with misundertandings and tension. These are the moments when managers face their worst workplace nightmares, often fearing any interaction with their teams, dreading that a misstep could jeopardize their jobs.

During stressful times, we tend to cling to our perspectives, sometimes unintentionally causing harm when trapped in the echo chambers of our beliefs. Nour Kteily, a professor at Northwestern's Kellogg School of Business, notes that psychological biases lie behind this behavior, including naive realism, which is "the bias to believe, 'I'm not biased. I believe that my view on the world is the correct view on the world, and anyone who disagrees with me isn't just a reasonable person who happened to see the world differently. It must be that they're cognitively biased, lazy, or just wrong.'"[13]

Clashes and difficult dialogues over unmet needs, differing expectations, and unresolved issues are inevitable in this ever-evolving world of complex work dynamics and polarizing politics. Those pulse-pounding, edge-of-your-seat, sometimes bonkers debates about who is right and wrong are just another day in the wild world of modern work. The key to handling these verbal duels is approaching them calmly, confidently, and empathetically without vilifying any side while trying to find solutions you can all agree on.

Effective leadership doesn't need to be a battle. Here are a few ways that managers can proactively practice conflict-resolution procedures aligned with their values:

- **Start Before Conflict Begins:** Kteily advocates for intentionally helping people think through disagreements, from political disputes to interpersonal conflicts, before they happen: "How do we express this agreement effectively? What are the appropriate channels by which to do so?" And to teach employees to identify potential bias in situations by asking themselves, "Which parts of that statement did I automatically disagree with?" and "How could I construct the best argument against my perspective if I had to?" Finally, Kteily recommends the practice of self-distancing, seeing conflicts from a neutral third-party perspective, which can promote an objective approach.[14]

- **Set Ground Rules:** Establish norms about acceptable behavior that aligns with your company values. Sample norms include:
  - Assume good intent.
  - One powerful voice at a time.
  - Find your growing edge and stay there.
  - Accept and expect lack of closure.
  - Empathy is not endorsement and understanding is not agreement, as I've learned from Jason Craige Harris, who has facilitated restorative justice conversations for several organizations I've been a part of.[15]

- **Embrace Restorative Justice Practices:** Seek to repair harm and rebuild trust in relationships through restorative justice practices that focus on acknowledging the harm from a miscommunication or hurtful statement, expressing remorse, admitting guilt, and committing to change through new policies, commitments, or agreements. In these moments, there's bound to be fear, hurt feelings, confusion, and a strong desire to be heard, understood, and validated, as people hold varying opinions, perspectives, and ideas. Haley Farrar of Aspen Restorative Consulting offers workshops on employing restorative processes, presenting the following conversation model:

1. **Ask for Permission:** Ask if the other person has time to talk and when would be convenient: "Do you have a moment to talk?" "When would be a good time to talk?"

2. **Include Affirmation:** Express appreciation for the person or something positive about the discussion: "I appreciate when you/ how you. . ."

3. **Understand the Issue:** Explain the incident or issue and its impact, seeking to understand what happened and what information is needed: "I want to talk to you about [name the incident/ issue] because [name one or two primary impacts on you]. What happened? What information do we both still need to know?"

4. **Identify Impacts:** Discuss the emotional and mental impact on both parties involved and others: "What is going on for you?" "How are you feeling about. . .?" "What are your thoughts on. . .?" "I've noticed the following impacts on myself and others. . . ."

5. **Identify Needs:** Determine the needs of each party in the conversation: "It sounds like you need. . .and I need. . ."

6. **Look for Repair:** Discuss the actions required to improve the situation: "What needs to happen to make this better?"

7. **Prevention:** Explore measures to prevent a recurrence: "What needs to happen to make sure this doesn't happen again?"

8. **Reach an Agreement:** Agree on resolutions and acknowledge them with gratitude: "What have we agreed on? Thank you!"[16]

Remember, burnout can manifest as defensiveness, irritability, and even low energy levels. Your team or colleagues may rely on you to be a steady, courageous, and wise presence, but your time, energy, and attention are finite resources. This is a long journey, so prioritize self-care and lean on others for support.

The workplace can be challenging, but we must extend grace to ourselves and others when mistakes happen. Many workplace nightmares stem from misunderstandings and assumptions about others' intentions. We should focus on self-awareness, understanding others, and practicing compassion to reduce these conflicts. The messy world of work will continue to test our empathy and energy, but by fostering these qualities, we can navigate it more effectively.

Surviving the Boiling Pot Syndrome

Imagine yourself in a pot of water, the temperature slowly rising. The tricky part is that you don't notice it because you're inside the pot, inviting others to join you and reassuring them that everything is just fine. Changes are occurring and the water is heating up steadily. This metaphor captures the experience of managers who struggle to recognize crucial signals of change within their organizations.

Change is a constant and sometimes unwelcome aspect of the business landscape. It can include economic fluctuations, structural transformations within your industry, leadership changes, or unexpected disruptions like the COVID-19 pandemic. When you're a manager, your role requires you to ensure your organization survives and thrives by effectively adapting to these ever-shifting circumstances.

The key here is spotting these changes and figuring out how to handle them. It's like a sneaky surprise party—not everyone gets the memo, and that can make things tricky. Sometimes leaders who are averse to conflict either deflect their responsibilities to HR or wait until the employee knows full well that their last days are counted to have the human conversation they should have had months prior.

Other times political infighting and deference to client or board relationships delay the sharing of critical information to employees, including what others really think of them. But in my experience it comes down to fear and lack of empathy shrouded in "I'm counting on you not saying anything because we're in the trenches together," or "Thank you for being such a good team player."

My learning journey, mirroring the basic principles of my meditation practice, has evolved into attentively observing my thoughts about people and situations. This has meant learning to step back from intense emotional reactions like fear, judgment, and outrage, and viewing them with curiosity instead of letting them take over like monkeys in my head.

For me, that also means acknowledging my tendency since childhood to please and care for others, often to the detriment of my health. I have the agency to choose how I respond to contentious remarks, unreasonable demands, or group tensions, preventing them from overpowering me.

It's one thing to aim for balance and another to achieve it. I've found that, like everything in life, regulating my emotions takes effort, patience, and the practice of being kind to both myself and others.

The real art lies in spotting emotional triggers early enough to prevent them from burning me to a crisp. While I don't always get it right, I make an effort to stay alert to early warning signs, such as growing irritability or feeling swamped due to mounting pressure, escalating conflicts within my team, or the creeping sense of overcommitment. When these signs start to emerge, here's what I do:

- When I notice my heart rate quickening and my breaths becoming shallower, I recognize these as cues to shift my focus.
- Instead of reacting to my emotions, I try to identify the specific stressors and the responses they trigger within me.
- I pause. Breathe. Check myself—my heart, mind, and body, and confirm whether what's happening around me is real or not. Only then do I take action.

Archetypes of Workplace Nightmares

Are you navigating the workplace of wild personalities? Amy Gallo's *Getting Along: How to Work with Anyone (Even Difficult People)* offers a guide to managing office archetypes that could otherwise turn your nine-to-five into a safari of workplace nightmares. She identifies eight common character types, providing insight into avoiding the stress traps and burnout burrows they might create:

1. The **Passive-Aggressive** type tops the list as one of the most common and frustrating. They might seem cooperative on the surface but then resist or undermine tasks indirectly, leaving their true intentions unclear.
2. The **Insecure Boss** can be a micromanager who constantly nitpicks, making you question your every move, or they might be overly paranoid and sabotage your career if they see you as a threat.
3. The **Pessimist** consistently highlights potential failures, often struggling to find anything positive to say.
4. The **Victim**, a variation of the pessimist, believes everyone is out to get them. They avoid taking responsibility and quickly blame others when things go wrong.

5. The **Know-It-All** is convinced they are the smartest person in the room, monopolizing conversations and confidently sharing misinformation.
6. The **Tormentor** climbed the career ladder through sacrifice but now mistreats those beneath them, turning what could have been a mentorship into a miserable experience.
7. The **Biased** individual knowingly or unknowingly engages in microaggressions, which can be inappropriate and harmful, regardless of their intent.
8. The **Political Operator** is solely focused on advancing their career, sometimes at the expense of others, displaying a ruthless approach to office politics.[17]

Gallo's book is like having a secret map to handle the wild side of office dynamics skillfully, helping nudge colleagues to healthier relationships, the bedrock of healthy communities at work.

Make Room to Learn from Others

I began writing weekly "Daisy updates" at Vice to share personal insights with my team. It was my way of sense-making for myself and them. But all management rituals deserve a check. When my direct reports suggested they take over these updates for more operational content, I embraced the change. Their team members enjoyed my notes, they kindly said, but they also wanted to hear operational updates directly from their team leaders.

Oh, and my notes were long!

I quickly shifted my focus away from the shame that inevitably arises when I feel I've messed up to focus on the team's growth. It wasn't about me. For over two years, I invited them in every week to learn and grow with me. I shared my reflections, flaws, advice, hopes, and aspirations, and now they asked to spread their leadership through their reflections. This is what happens when you build a culture of psychological safety!

I wanted to show up for my team with deep gratitude so I asked, "How can I help?" Their response was "Nothing, we've got this." When people feel they belong, are connected, and are included in decision-making, they welcome opportunities to contribute their ideas and best efforts.

This inclusivity doesn't just look good on paper; it's awe-inspiring.

This shift taught me a valuable lesson about adaptability and openness in leadership. It wasn't just about sharing my experiences but also about making room for others to express themselves and contribute their perspectives. The team's involvement transformed our updates into a dynamic and inclusive platform, reflecting a diversity of styles and personal stories.

My team's response was inspiring. They designed a format and schedule, infusing their unique personalities into each update. Every Monday, I eagerly awaited the "HR Update," now enriched by my team's voices and experiences, offering fresh insights and strengthening our work culture.[18]

Even in the best jobs, it's typical to question yourself and your abilities, even why you work where you do. As your role becomes more complex, you'll encounter increasingly demanding challenges and people, often requiring heightened levels of determination to get through. Constantly confronting new hurdles and learning experiences can be draining, potentially leading to job dissatisfaction and burnout. Additionally, the fast-paced nature of today's world can feel overwhelming, requiring moments of pause and reflection.

Remember, you hold the power to transform work nightmares into opportunities for personal and professional development. This transformation can lead to enhanced self-awareness, better decision-making, and increased resilience. Prioritizing self-care and self-repair can turn your work nightmares into epic adventures and help you find your sense of awe at work.

Let the Sparks Fly: How We Grow

This chapter focused on rediscovering the joy in our work, reigniting the initial spark of enthusiasm and passion you once had, and cultivating a culture of generosity, empathy, and an abundance mindset. The goal is to see and embrace each other's humanity, working collaboratively to build and create more extraordinary things together. Now let's consider these scripts to help you let go of what's not meant for you and light your way forward for you and your team.

Scripts for Managers and Teams

Managers:

- "I would like us to channel joy, hope, and optimism in our work. Can you share when you felt most energized and most drained this week?"
- "My viewpoint could be incomplete. Is there another way to view this situation or project?"
- "To manage this hectic period effectively, let's agree on three main priorities. This will help us concentrate on what's most crucial and avoid wearing ourselves out by just being busy."
- "I'm here to help you. If you're feeling scattered, overwhelmed, or frustrated, let's work together to find a solution."

Teams:

- "I have ideas about [project/task] that might improve our approach. Can we schedule a time to discuss?"
- "I'm eager to learn more about this initiative. Can you help me understand [concept/task] better?"
- "I'm feeling overwhelmed due to the political tensions within our team. Could we explore strategies to handle this more effectively?"
- "I've been struggling with some past experiences impacting my work. Can we talk about possible support or accommodations?"

Remember, managers can transform work nightmares into personal and professional growth opportunities through self-awareness, empathy, and balancing professional productivity with emotional well-being.

Let's use our beginner's mind and get started!

7

Get Right Within: Become the Manager Every Team Deserves

"I'm going to be mediocre today."

During a check-in with one of my direct reports, she opened up about her struggles with an expanding workload. This conversation came at a tumultuous time for our company amid tough economic conditions and challenging employee expectations. On top of her demanding job, she was also juggling a busy home life, caring for two children, one with special needs. Despite my efforts to lighten her load by shifting deadlines and suggesting the possibility of a break, her anxiety was intensifying.

In a moment of candidness, I confessed, "Some days, I just tell myself, 'I'm going to be mediocre today.' It's not about underperforming, but about easing the pressure off myself." This idea of embracing mediocrity, not as a sign of weakness but as a mental and emotional shield, seemed to click with her. We shared a knowing smile and decided to aim for our "mediocre best," understanding that it was a mental and emotional respite strategy, not a compromise of our standards.

And we joked that our output likely surpassed others even on these so-called mediocre days.

When the world seemed intent on burning us out, we had agency to say, "not today." This strategy stemmed from my journey as a high-achieving woman of color. Why stop at 100% when you can crank it up at 110% and leave absolutely no room for doubt about why I should be the one climbing that ladder? Always going the extra mile, even when my tank was empty, living by a famous line from *Hamilton*, "I'm an immigrant. I get the job done."[1] As a Latina, I learned from my Black mentors and friends about the harsh reality of needing to "work twice as hard to get half as far."[2] However, each step forward in my career often came with a significant toll on my health and well-being.

In a professional world rife with imposter syndrome and overwhelming societal pressures shaped by misogyny and racism, embracing temporary— and relative—"mediocrity" became a vital survival strategy. It enabled me to support my teams effectively without enduring constant sacrifices. This approach gave me room to step back, breathe, and recalibrate. It was a strategic pause, allowing me to show up as my best self without falling prey to the relentless burnout cycle.

In this chapter, we're diving into the art and science of being the best version of ourselves for our teams. I offer insights and tips on becoming the manager we aspire to be—the kind of leader each of us has the potential to become. It's about embracing those moments of lightness, grace, and even a dash of mediocrity as secret ingredients for sustained excellence and personal well-being.

A Guide to Mediocrity

Embracing the notion of a "mediocre" day as a self-care tool can be a surprisingly effective way to ease the weight of life and work stressors. Let me share with you how I worked on the art of "not doing the most" when I managed a global team:

- **A Slower Start:** Aim to begin mornings not with the usual rush to emails (what disaster awaits me?), but with a peaceful ritual of meditation, yoga, or strength training, followed by a soothing cup of tea. This tranquil start sets the tone for the rest of the day.

- **Trimming Down the "Must-Dos":** Select only three critical tasks for the day. Rather than being a slave to the constant ding of emails and texts, prioritize these three tasks. This breathing space wasn't just for me; it also encouraged others to independently tackle those less urgent issues, fostering a sense of autonomy.
- **Slowing My Roll Throughout the Day:** Resist the typical subway sprint for a more leisurely stride, experimenting with new routes to and from work and around the office. This gentler, more exploratory approach lets you take in new surroundings, offering a refreshing change to the usual hustle.

To be fair, I didn't achieve these 100% of the time. As with any practice, it took time and a fair bit of trial and error. It's about intentionally stepping back from the constant buzz and letting some things simmer on their own.

What would adopting a "mediocre" day look like for you?

Getting Right Within

In today's fast-paced world, a workplace that prioritizes mental and physical health, work-life balance, and team well-being is not just ideal; it's essential for thriving. I firmly believe that it's entirely possible to master the art of managing people without dampening their spirits. This belief aligns with Lauryn Hill's lyrics "How you gonna win when you ain't right within?"[3] These words echo the fundamental truth that effective management starts with self-awareness and nurturing our inner selves.

Only when we're aligned and at peace within can we truly inspire and lead others.

In the demanding world of leadership, taking care of our well-being is not just optional; it's necessary. Remember, if you don't take a break, your body will choose the least convenient time to take it. The secret to creating high-performance teams and avoiding burnout is prioritizing well-being—starting with you.

Throughout this book, I've detailed the impact of burnout on our teams. Employee well-being is suffering more than ever. I can't say this enough: As managers, we can influence how people feel. This means we can either exacerbate or mitigate burnout.

This chapter, however, is about you. To truly understand ourselves, we must confront the broken parts we often shy away from acknowledging, even to ourselves.

My journey underscored the importance of confronting deep-seated inner conflicts. Raised by my paternal grandparents, I struggled with deep-seated feelings of abandonment since my mother was not present in my life from the age of two. Despite being deeply loved, I found myself in the "good girl" role, navigating my grandmother's emotional swings and my grandfather's indiscretions while simultaneously pushing myself academically to gain their approval. This early role as a mediator not only shaped my character but also influenced my approach to management, where I've always strived to uphold harmony and positivity.

In adulthood, this pattern manifested in my relationships, often leading me into manipulative situations, stemming from my own insecurities about self-worth. It wasn't until my 50s that I began to confront these long-suppressed insecurities, engaging in therapy and heartfelt discussions with my family. Opening up about my vulnerabilities to my husband and daughter was a turning point, leading me to understand that my professional ambitions were not solely about personal achievement but also about making up for my mother's absence and validating the love I received from my father's family.

This realization brought about a profound healing. I came to see that much of my career had been, albeit unconsciously, an attempt to mend the hurt I had experienced. Acknowledging this was pivotal in reshaping my leadership approach. I realized that I didn't need to turn myself inside out to create healthy and sustainable workplaces. It further reinforced the importance of being internally aligned to effectively guide and support others.

Integrating these personal revelations into my professional life, I've honed a leadership style that prioritizes empathy, candor, reflection, and well-being. This approach has improved my effectiveness in managing teams, allowing me to embrace and share my strengths in a manner that nourishes and unlocks the potential of others. It reflects the type of leader I aspire to be, the kind I longed for at different stages of my career, and the kind of leader I believe you, too, can become.

Women of Color and Burnout

"What does it mean that a Black, lesbian, feminist, warrior, poet, mother is named the state poet of New York? It means that we live in a world full of the most intense contradictions. And we must find ways to use the best we have—ourselves, our work—to bridge those contradictions; to learn the lessons that those contradictions teach. And that is the work of the poet within each one of us: to envision what has not yet been and to work with every fiber of who we are to make the reality pursuit of those visions irresistible."[4]

These are Audre Lorde's poignant words from the documentary *A Litany for Survival: The Life and Work of Audre Lorde.* As the poet laureate of New York during the early '90s, Lorde spoke about her complex identity against the backdrop of the era's civil and cultural upheavals.

Lorde's wisdom lies in the idea that by embracing life's contradictions through the lens of our unique identities, we have the power to envision and mold futures that have yet to be explored.

If you're a woman in a management role, you likely shoulder the dual responsibility of caring for your well-being and that of your family, loved ones, and employees. Fueled by a mix of grit and grace, you've mastered the art of keeping everything afloat amid the messy and chaotic. It's an immense burden to shoulder.

In a LinkedIn post on November 8, 2023, Stephanie Nadi Olson, CEO of We Are Rosie, a flexible career platform for marketers, shared how being a founder and CEO had taken a toll on her. Nadi Olson said, "Since transitioning out of CEO at We Are Rosie, my cholesterol is down 25 points. I've lost 30 pounds. I've stopped taking anxiety medication. I loved my job and loved putting my heart and soul into it. That hasn't changed. But I want to be really open about the health implications of this work and encourage people to take a break. We're not designed to be operating at 100%, 100% of the time."[5]

This recurring theme again resonated when, at a premiere of the film *Flamin' Hot,* I heard Annie Gonzalez, who portrayed the resilient wife in the movie, capture the essence of the women of color experience: "In our communities, we are either the soft landing or the iron fist, constantly moving between the two."[6] Her observation speaks to the complex, often contrasting roles women of color navigate in personal and professional spheres.

This continuous balancing act is not just exhausting; it's unsustainable.

Women of color in the workforce face a host of challenges: excessive workloads, high-pressure problem-solving demands, isolation, microaggressions, and exclusion. These issues are often neglected. Additionally, there are the mental acrobatics and the need to put on a mask to make other people feel comfortable, consistently "going high" when others go low.[7] As managers, we hold a unique position to give voice to these often unspoken struggles, advocating for ourselves and those we lead. It's our responsibility as managers to highlight and address these persistent issues, championing change where it's needed most, and building capacity of leadership to understand and manage grief, overwhelm, and burnout.

Here are a few strategies to support women of color in the workplace:

- **Speak Up:** Voice your support for women of color, using your privilege to advocate for them. Be explicit in your endorsements. Say, "I show support for [name] because [reason]."
- **Raise Awareness:** It takes more than reading a book or two to show up for women of color truly; you can start by educating yourself. Explore and share insightful books like Ruchika Tulshyan's *Inclusion on Purpose*[8], *Right Within* by Minda Harts or Deepa Purushothaman's *The First, the Few, the Only.*[9]
- **Open Doors:** Actively create opportunities for women of color by making introductions and advocating for their inclusion on teams and speaking opportunities, even if it means stepping aside yourself.
- **Persist:** Tackle biases, confront microaggressions, and address exclusion head-on. When faced with budget cuts for diversity, equity, and inclusion efforts, prioritize funding for the remaining essential work. Hold managers accountable when they resist engaging in difficult conversations about hostile behavior or racial and gender inequity.

To women of color, I say this: Hold on to your magic, your secret sauce. Protect it, rest and replenish when necessary, and lean on others for support. Our friendships and connections can be generative, nourishing, and sustaining.[10]

We can all break down barriers by actively supporting women of color, educating ourselves, creating opportunities, and challenging the status quo. This commitment fosters an inclusive and equitable future and cultivates the supportive environment essential for the leaders we so desperately need, leaders who are vital for the thriving of others.

Define the Manager You Want to Be

Who you are is how you lead. To become the manager you are capable of becoming, you need to know yourself. Ultimately, it comes down to defining the kind of leader you want to be: one who shines a light on others or dims it.

Let's start with self-awareness, the bedrock of effective management.

Understanding our strengths, limitations, emotions, and triggers is critical to making informed choices and fostering healthy team dynamics. Daniel Goleman emphasizes the importance of emotional intelligence in the workplace, often outweighing technical skills.[11] Emotional intelligence, emphasizing empathy, vulnerability, and authenticity, is critical for creating a dynamic and trusting workplace culture. This approach can strengthen team bonds, boost productivity, and cultivate a positive and engaging work environment.

In high-pressure work environments, where the emphasis is on "doing more with less" and achieving agility and rapid results, phrases like "We need faster results. Get your people under control, and don't jeopardize our narrative to the market" and "Stop complaining, get shit done" often exacerbate team stress and morale problems. This relentless drive for efficiency and quick outcomes can significantly strain both teams and their leaders.

During a SALA Series panel discussion moderated by Mori Taheripour, a negotiation expert and Wharton professor, with Arielle Patrick, chief communications officer at Ariel Investments, and Mark Tatum, deputy commissioner and chief operating officer for the National Basketball Association, we explored balancing employee, leader, and market demands. Mori reminded me of the opening quote from my TEDx Talk, "Inclusion Revolution," featuring my father's wisdom: "M'ija, keep your head down and work harder than everyone else." She asked, "Would you offer the same advice today?"

My response remained unwavering: "Yes—hard work is irreplaceable, and the roadmap to career resilience is rooted in 'getting things done.' However, it must coexist with owning our magic—our unique identities, experiences, talents, and aspirations propel us forward." I highlighted that the essence of effective leadership lies in understanding our core values.[12]

My calling here isn't about shrinking to fit but standing confidently in our truth. Defining your leadership style is not just about coping with what you're given; it's about unlocking your best self.

Here's a little secret: Your team doesn't expect you to be perfect. They need you to be present and supportive. Your role is less about maintaining a facade of flawlessness and more about seeking self-awareness, being receptive to feedback, adapting, and, most importantly, caring genuinely for your team.

What does your best management self look like?

Management Archetypes

After carefully studying and analyzing different ways of managing, I've identified five main management archetypes:

1. **The Servant Manager:** Builds trust and encourages individual empowerment, team collaboration, and growth. This approach can seem time-consuming or too lenient and weak in certain cultures.[13]

2. **The Transformational Manager:** Rallies teams around bold, meaningful, and challenging objectives, sparking considerable change and innovation within the organization. Plays a crucial role in unlocking the potential for large-scale transformation or accelerating change.[14]

3. **The Transactional Manager:** Prioritizes performance and decision-making, especially in short-term projects and crises, but may hold back healthy relationships and innovation.[15]

4. **The Micromanager:** Overbearing, hinders creativity and team morale by not empowering team members. If you're not empowering your team, you're asking them to check out mentally.[16]

5. **The Neglectful Manager:** Disengaged, leading to mistrust, organizational stagnation, and morale issues. A lack of presence and/or abandonment mark this archetype, as well as unclear guidance, no feedback or recognition, not being available or willing to address employee concerns, and decision-making paralysis.[17]

Understand and match your management style to what you're good at, and what brings you joy. See management as a continuous, flexible journey of learning. Adapt your approach to stay true to your best self, connect with your team and achieve your group's goals.

Sprinkle Gratitude and Joy Like Confetti

Simple activities like the "Confetti" tradition my board colleague Maneesh Goyal[18] initiated at Planned Parenthood Federation of America board meetings can create meaningful connections. This practice involves sharing personal photos and updates at the start of meetings. This heartwarming activity, often filled with shared laughter, is a delightful way to learn about each other and strengthen bonds.

So here's a little trick to sprinkle care around like confetti:

> Think of that person who's been a superhero, swooping in when you needed them most. Or maybe it's that quiet soul who did something small yet unforgettable. And what about your mentor or sponsor, the one who gets you? They opened doors you didn't even know existed or saved you from walking into disaster zones.
>
> Now, here's a wild idea—say "thank you." And I mean, craft a thank-you that's so thoughtful it deserves an award. Let it be a tribute to their awesomeness.

One afternoon, I received a delightful surprise at home while feeling under the weather: a beautiful bouquet of white flowers. The accompanying note said, "I emailed you and you accepted without hesitation. For that I'm grateful." This unexpected gesture of appreciation was the perfect pick-me-up.

The real magic here? You shine a little light into the world, making it a smidge more lovely, and weaving together our patchwork community. All because you took a moment to sprinkle your gratitude.

Find Your Why

After giving a keynote speech on belonging and connection at work for Seramount, where I shared my early life experiences and highlighted a profound question from Esther Armah, CEO of the Armah Institute of Emotional Justice – "Who are you, and whose are you?" – to emphasize the importance of understanding what and who shapes us, I was delighted to receive a heart-felt message from Sam Ushio, founder of Connect 3x. "Your story represents the very best in an intentional ikigai journey!"

Ikigai is a Japanese concept roughly translated as "a reason for being," or your true life purpose, satisfaction, and fulfillment. This concept suggests that you can unearth a sense of meaning and contentment by aligning your passions, talents, and values, and addressing the world's needs. In a thought-provoking episode of the *In the Arena* podcast, featuring Leah Smart and Tim Tamashiro, author of *How to Ikigai: Lessons for Finding Happiness and Living Your Life's Purpose,* Tim beautifully describes it as "the inherent gifts you possess, which you can naturally share with others, thus illuminating and enriching their lives."[19]

The next time you struggle with finding your calling, or your reason to jump out of bed in the morning, try finding your ikigai by reflecting on these questions:[20]

- What activities and pursuits bring you joy and enthusiasm? This helps you determine what you love (your passion).
- What skills and talents do you possess for the greater good? This helps you determine what you are good at (your calling).
- In what ways can you be acknowledged and rewarded for your contributions to the world? This helps you determine what you can be rewarded for (your profession).
- How can you make a positive impact on others and the world at large? This helps you determine what the world needs (your mission).

Drawing nearer to your ikigai, that elusive sweet spot where your life's purpose is fully realized, can influence your perspective on work and lighten the unbearable weight of structures and systems designed to burn us out. It's the fuel that keeps your fire burning, your reason to grin at every curveball thrown your way. By staying true to your purpose, you'll unleash the talent within, ignite your inner drive, and succeed like never before.

How might aligning with your purpose enrich how you interact with your teams and influence your professional decisions?

Discover the Power of "Why": Unleashing Positive Energy at Work

We thrive at work when we align our passion with our team's and organizations' mission, igniting a unique energy—let's call it "good vibes." This is more than just feeling incredible; it's about channeling that positivity into productivity. Imagine this energy as the joy of an impromptu party celebrating you, representing our thirst for belonging and being part of something larger than us. When we're in sync with our "why," our motivation skyrockets and our work shines. It's crucial to understand what fuels this fire and what dampens it.

It's easy to lose sight of our "why" amid routine chaos, concentrating solely on immediate tasks. It can feel like being stuck on a merry-go-round of distractions. To break free from this repetitive cycle, it's beneficial to reflect on those illuminating moments that firmly root us in our true purpose.

Remember that excitement when you landed your first job or first high-profile assignment? These aren't just throwback moments—they're our personal "why" GPS, guiding us through life's choppy waters. They're like nostalgic postcards, reminding us why we started this wild ride in the first place and what keeps our engines revving.

I had a "why" revelation when my daughter asked what I did every day at work. Seeing aspects of yourself that you typically overlook through someone else's perspective can be wild. As I described my responsibilities—from overseeing the entire employee lifecycle (recruitment, onboarding, development, retention, exit) to stabilizing teams and unlocking manager potential to leading cross-functional projects and advocating for equity and belonging—I realized my role as a guardian of our global teams' communal energy. My job was about ensuring smooth work dynamics while building the capacity of leaders to understand humans in their full complexity. This is my "why," the driving force behind my impact.

This realization or awakening reaffirms that our "why" is always within us, ready to light the path and inspire.

Embrace your "why," and watch the magic happen in your work and relationships.

Discover Your Rest Needs

In *Sacred Rest: Recover Your Life, Renew Your Energy, Restore Your Sanity,* Dr. Saundra Dalton-Smith presents a comprehensive approach to rest, challenging the conventional focus on sleep. As a board-certified internal medicine physician, she emphasizes the need for a holistic rest regimen encompassing seven distinct types: physical, mental, spiritual,

(continued)

(continued)

emotional, social, sensory, and creative. Dr. Dalton-Smith's work highlights that to feel fully alive and authentic, one must cater to each of
these areas. Each type of rest has unique characteristics and potential
deficits, manifesting in various ways: for example, body aches from
inadequate physical rest, lack of meaning and connection at work
from a lack of spiritual rest, or suppressed emotions from insufficient
emotional rest. Sound familiar? Dr. Dalton-Smith's insights offer practical strategies for individuals to identify and fulfill their specific rest
needs, helping to prevent burnout and promoting a balanced and fulfilling life.[21]

In her holistic well-being approach, Dr. Dalton-Smith also created a unique rest quiz (https://www.restquiz.com/quiz/rest-quiz-
test/) to help identify the most significant areas of rest deficit. This
tool allows anyone to pinpoint which of the seven types of rest they
are most lacking. By highlighting the areas where one's "rest muscles"
are weakest, the quiz offers a starting point for focusing on one or two
specific rest types and employing small, targeted, and achievable personal restorative practices.

Build Your Refuge

Leading people can often feel like a unforgiving solitary and lonely journey,
one that can easily lead to burnout, but it doesn't have to be that way.
Sometimes it means asking for help and accepting it when offered.

During a severe period of burnout that triggered skin and stomach
issues, I continued to show up at work as if everything was normal. Then,
one day, at the end of a one-on-one check-in, a senior leader on my team
asked with concern, "Daisy, are you OK?" I paused and internally did the
mental calculation of what I could share without diminishing her spirits.
I breathed heavily and managed to reply, "I'm going to be OK; it's just a
tough time right now," fighting back tears. She looked so sad as she
responded, "The team is talking about how worried they are for you. I don't
know what to tell them. But please let me know if I can help."

This moment forced me to look in the mirror, and I found my reflection
unsettling. I was grateful for her concern, but I was equally concerned about

the ripple effect of my stress and health issues on the team. As I shared in Chapter 1, this incident, coupled with the overwhelming burden of pain and burnout, led me to seek help from doctors, a nutritionist, an acupuncturist, and finally, a personal trainer. I set out to create a network of support to restore my health and balance, project managing myself back to health. The next step involved reevaluating my work-related needs: finding purpose, seeking a sense of community, and prioritizing wellness. In essence, this meant creating my own refuge.

I've found that creating various forms of safe havens in the workplace can help address the challenges and personal crises managers face in the modern workplace, especially in the context of work and personal identity.

Admitting you need a helping hand, a refuge in others, is vital. Yet it raises a question: *How often do we signal for help? And how often do we accept help when it is offered?*

At times, our refuge appears unexpectedly.

Over the course of my career I have learned that the importance of replenishing one's cup cannot be overstated. My friend Alison Turkos, an activist, author, and advocate, once sent me a note when some rather tough press about our company was circulating. Her message was a potent reminder of an essential truth: "Remember, you can't pour from an empty cup." That day, her words hit me hard. I was so drained that even a sliver of energy seemed beyond reach. Overwhelmed by the internal strains of managing a public crisis, I couldn't even muster the strength to ask for help. Yet, in her intuitive way, Alison sensed my need. Her gesture was like a release valve for the stress and anxiety I had accumulated.

Sometimes, I've found refuge in the insights of experts who lift me up with clarity and courage when I need it most.

In my office, I surround myself with inspirational quotes, one of which is from theologian Howard Thurman: "Don't ask yourself what the world needs. Ask yourself what makes you come alive, and go do that, because what the world needs is people who have come alive."[22] This quote lights me up whenever I feel overwhelmed or powerless in the face of numerous work pressures. It prompts me to consider what energizes me and to take a moment to recalibrate before succumbing to the all-too-familiar mix of exhaustion, cynicism, and inefficiency that leads to burnout. Adopting this viewpoint reminds me that by being fully present, engaged, and lit up, I can show my team the value of doing work that is not only necessary but also personally meaningful.

Referring to shame as the intensely painful feeling or experience of believing that we are unworthy of love and belonging, Brené Brown says, "The less you talk about it, the more you got it. Shame needs three things to grow exponentially in our lives: secrecy, silence, and judgment."[23]

Sometimes we have to silence our inner critic, the voice of shame, and build our own refuge.

Recharge by Pressing Pause

In a world constantly in motion, taking a step back can be a radical act. Organizational psychologist Adam Grant echoed this sentiment in a social media post on August 17, 2021, affirming that it is OK, necessary, and beneficial to rest, relax, take breaks, and play:

Resting is not a waste of time. It's an investment in well-being.
Relaxing is not a sign of laziness. It's a source of energy.
Breaks are not a distraction. They're a chance to refocus attention.
Play is not a frivolous activity. It's a path to connection and creativity.[24]

Throughout my career, I've experienced a mix of rewarding and somber moments in the workplace. I've had the pleasure of contributing to admired companies, influencing changes in equity practices, and fostering inclusive environments. However, I've also witnessed and personally endured the extra challenges employees face, particularly women and people of color. These aren't just typical job struggles, including emotional burnout and systemic obstacles to career progression, leading to an oppressive and demoralizing work environment.

The value of rest, often overlooked in our hustle culture, is a critical component of productivity. It's a catalyst for creativity, efficiency, and focus. So how do we integrate rest into corporate culture?

Sometimes we have to pause.

On August 16, the day after leaving my position as Vice's global chief people officer, I announced my radical sabbatical on LinkedIn.[25] The outpouring of support and understanding I received highlighted a shared sense of burnout and a curiosity about the nourishing power of sabbaticals.

My decision to take a sabbatical emerged from discussions with my executive coach, Rha Goddess, about the depletion I felt from leading through prolonged uncertainty and instability. The term "radical sabbatical" was inspired by Rolando Brown, a client of Rha's, who had coined the phrase for his sabbatical a year prior. After years of enduring what seemed like a never-ending health crisis, providing emotional support to peers, teammates, and colleagues, all while tackling a gazillion new challenges that blurred the lines between personal struggles and work responsibilities without any guidebook—I realized that had led me to a state of prolonged burnout, unlike anything I'd ever encountered in my career.

Recognizing that I had neglected myself for too long, I knew I deserved to take a breather, a chance to reevaluate, and an opportunity to let revelations flow. I yearned for a *refugio*—a sanctuary for serenity, reflection, and action where I could pour onto myself what I needed most to feel whole, healthy, joyful, and safe.

Although my decision was deeply personal, it was also evidence-based.[26] Articles and employee surveys have unveiled a widespread feeling of burnout and disengagement within the traditional nine-to-five work grind, with more than 40% of workers reporting demotivation.[27] Insights from research by BambooHR underscore employee unhappiness has reached a new peak since 2020. The underlying causes of this widespread workplace discontent can be attributed to the lingering health and economic ramifications of the COVID-19 pandemic, and messy layoffs, budget cuts, and office return mandates.[28]

Once I committed to a radical sabbatical, Rha posed three essential questions that helped me design my path:

1. What would need to be handled for you to slow down?
2. If you could slow down, what could be possible for you that isn't right now?
3. As you consider taking this time in service of "what's next," what will you need to make this radical sabbatical truly awesome?

Everyone's sabbatical path is unique; some seek grand faraway adventures, leaving behind daily routines. Others tailor their sabbaticals to focus on learning new skills or hobbies that ignite their passions. In a previous sabbatical five years ago, I whisked my family away on travel adventures, volunteered with causes near to my heart, and dreamed up a more expansive vision of my next career move.

Answering these questions led me to engage in activities that brought me joy and healing during this period. This included speaking engagements, my happiness hack, and writing, a therapeutic outlet. I also embraced wellness retreats, drawing inspiration from Audre Lorde's view of self-care as an act of self-preservation.[29] They became a profound means of reclamation, a deliberate step toward nurturing myself in anticipation of what lies ahead.

To make this sabbatical meaningful, I adopted this practice:

1. **Create a Routine:** Limit of three scheduled daily activities, allowing space for essential commitments.
2. **Give It Meaning:** Categorize activities as Generative, Nourishing, or Restful, depending on their purpose. Only engage in activities that fit these categories.
3. **Keep Intentions Sacred:** Regularly reminded myself to honor the purpose of this sabbatical.

Reflective inquiries have always been a part of my approach, helping me navigate life's complexities. During my sabbatical, I kept a journal and a repository of my social media posts entitled "Radical Sabbatical Chronicles," which helped me share and make sense of my experience. The following questions were on my reflection rotation:

- How do I want to show up in the world?
- What do I want my work and career to be about?
- How can I continue to channel joy, hope, and optimism as I heal from my deepest wounds?
- What do I need this moment to be for me so that I can remain awake and open to the possibilities?

On days when I felt wobbly and doubted my journey, decisions, or the current moment, I would ask myself reflective questions: "What's holding you back?" "What's blocking your path, whether real or imagined?" and "What do you want more of?" These questions helped me navigate trying periods and inspired my social media posts and the writing of this book. They served as a valuable tool for self-discovery and expression.

Treating work and career breaks as closely guarded secrets or topics shrouded in taboos was not on the menu. One important realization was the need to address the stigma surrounding career breaks. As reported in Forbes, many people, especially executives, are reluctant to discuss their sabbaticals with potential employers.[30] It's time to change this narrative and advocate for more flexible workplace policies.

My vision for my sabbatical was to carve out a personal path of rest, recovery, and reflection. It was an opportunity to redefine my life's next chapter with intention. I invite you to consider embarking on your self-care, meditation, and growth journey. We can shed light on the unspoken, mend our wounds, and boldly rewrite the stories of our lives with purpose and intention.[31]

Mind Your Hara Hachi Bu Point

In the world of management, we can draw a valuable lesson from the Japanese concept of *hara hachi bu,* which means "Eat until you're 80% full."[32] This practice, deeply rooted in Okinawan culture, has been a guiding principle for maintaining healthy eating habits and longevity. It's not just about food; it's a mindful approach to life.

Imagine beginning every day at work with a reminder akin to *hara hachi bu,* a simple phrase that prompts you to pause and reflect before diving into the day's challenges. Much like Okinawans thoughtfully manage their meals, we, as managers, can manage our responses.

To apply this wisdom in a professional context, consider resetting your mental muscle memory. Most of us are taught that leadership requires us to respond quickly and assertively. Instead of reacting impulsively in moments of crisis or high-pressure situations, try pausing, taking a step back, and assessing your thoughts and physical responses. Try asking: What scares or angers me at this moment? What do we need to solve for now? What can wait? How do I want to show up for myself and my team?

Research has shown that slowing down our breath helps reduce fears and anxieties and helps you tap into your brain more clearly, thereby managing your thoughts, moods, and experiences.[33] Tempering our reactions without sacrificing our capacity to express care can be profoundly liberating and loving.

In the same way *hara hachi bu* encourages smaller portions, we can encourage more measured responses. By doing so, we promote a more thoughtful, deliberate management style and create a work environment where employees feel valued and heard. Just as Okinawans have achieved remarkable health and longevity through this practice, we, as managers, can foster healthier workplace dynamics and build lasting relationships with our teams. It's a brilliant approach that transcends cultural boundaries and speaks to the heart of effective leadership.

This analogy resonates with what I've learned from positive psychology, a field that delves into enhancing the human condition, our well-being, through engagement, relationships, meaning, and accomplishment, starting with self-awareness and evolving into self-compassion.[34] When applied to management, these principles cultivate an emotionally resilient mindset, prioritizing individual and collective well-being. I think of it as a holistic leadership approach that ensures that you and your team not only shine but do so sustainably, living and working gently, and avoiding burnout.

Wellness Loop

Nedra Tawwab, therapist and author, often shares profound mental health insights, such as "No one talks about how exhausting it is to pretend to be OK. Moving through your day while grieving, sad, angry, anxious, depressed, etc., requires a lot of effort." Persistent pretending can drain the qualities vital for a healthy organization: creativity, collaboration, and productivity, not to mention its toll on personal well-being and the all-too-common road to burnout.

Managing overwhelming workloads, market pressures, interpersonal conflicts, and misuse of power at work while also facing personal struggles is a daunting task. Admitting to my direct reports, as I occasionally did during the pandemic, "Today I'm not OK and might not be at my best," was my way of being transparent and acknowledging that we all have bad days. Each time, I was met with understanding rather than judgment or ridicule.

Here's an approach to personal and interpersonal well-being that combines several positive psychology principles:

1. **Self-Awareness:** It all starts here, and it kicks off with tuning in to your thoughts, emotions, and actions. Through self-reflection practices like journaling and mindfulness, you lay the groundwork for your growth.

2. **Self-Compassion:** It's about treating yourself with the same kindness and understanding you'd offer to a good friend, especially when the going gets tough. A trio of self-kindness, a sense of shared human experiences, and mindfulness form the bedrock of this approach.[35]

3. **Self-Care:** The Self-Care Wheel, a tool popularized by positive psychology, helps you assess areas of your life—mental, emotional, spiritual, personal, professional, and physical. It's designed to help you identify where you're struggling, merely coping, or excelling, enabling you to develop a focused strategy to enhance areas that require more attention.[36]

4. **Awareness of Others:** Here, you tune in to what others are going through, cultivating interpersonal empathy and a deeper understanding that everyone faces difficulties.

5. **Compassion for Others:** This is where we embrace our collective human experience, fostering compassion and connection of diverse viewpoints and experiences. It involves techniques to release the need for external validation, focusing instead on genuine interpersonal support.

6. **Care for Others:** This is where the magic of self-compassion and self-care extends beyond yourself, positively impacting how you interact with, lead, and care for others.

Please think of this as an interconnected loop of activity that we go through repeatedly, enhancing personal and interpersonal well-being and safeguarding against burnout. Connecting our awareness and care for ourselves with awareness and care for others makes us better people leaders.

Seek Empathy

My favorite take on empathy comes from Mohsin Hamid, a Pakistani novelist, who said, "Empathy is about finding echoes of another person in yourself."[37] If we take a plunge into understanding each other's beliefs and values, a whole world of feeling seen is waiting for us. It's like opening doors to each other's inner worlds and finding out, hey, we're not so different after all.

We can lay the groundwork for more profound, more meaningful connections by embracing each other's humanity, including our most guarded vulnerabilities. Understanding and accepting our vulnerabilities begins with showing empathy for ourselves. This self-empathy is essential to building authentic, compassionate relationships within and outside the workplace.

In other words, empathy isn't just a nice-to-have; it's a bridge-builder, a gap-mender. It enhances our understanding of one another and paves the way for relationships that are not just bearable but harmonious. But it's hard to lean into empathy when you're in the thick of it.

I once found myself in a "reached my limits" conversation with my manager that stretched my empathy muscles, and altered our relationship and my leadership.

The incident stemmed from an insensitive racial remark made by a white male executive during a team meeting. His comments sent shockwaves through the team, igniting a passionate demand to mend and rectify the hurt he had inflicted. I was swiftly called upon to facilitate what I framed as a restorative justice conversation.

As we were gearing up to move forward, an unforeseen complication arose: a former employee took to Instagram, leaking the executive's comment along with his image and quote. This development rapidly escalated the situation, drawing in the head of public relations and communications.

There was no sidestepping the reality of what had been said; denial or deflection was not an option. This moment called for applying the management approach I've emphasized, balancing empathy with a frank understanding of the necessary steps ahead. When the executive, concerned about his reputation, sought my advice, my response was kind and straightforward: "I get that you're feeling uneasy about this. But you said it. We can't make it go away. Let's give this situation some time to cool down. I strongly recommend holding off on any public responses, as it will only make matters worse." This advice wasn't just about damage control but about taking responsible and ethical actions in response to the unfolding events.

In an effort to move beyond a superficial, reluctant admission of wrongdoing, I proposed several suggestions to my boss, who was also this executive's manager. These suggestions included coaching and disciplinary actions, such as unpaid leave. Her response took me aback: "You've always been biased against him," she said. "I need this to be resolved, and I need you to handle it." Her tone left no room for further discussion; these were her explicit instructions.

What troubled me deeply was realizing that a white woman, who knew me well, was asking me—a Latina—to prioritize a white man's self-preservation for the company's sake despite the harm he inflicted. I interpreted this directive as an undermining of my identity, values, and expertize, triggering feelings of invalidation and moral injury, a traumatic response to actions that contradict deeply held beliefs.[38] Painfully, I complied, tasked with balancing caring for the white manager and addressing the needs of the affected employees.

This was not my first experience with moral conflict in leading people, where my integrity and values were tested in navigating uncomfortable truths. However, as my relationship with my manager was fracturing, the burden of not being able to fully heal these employees' emotional distress and feelings of unsafety, factors known to drive trauma and burnout, weighed heavily on my conscience and emotions.

In our lives, we assume various roles, sometimes causing harm or being harmed. Yet we also possess the power to heal and extend grace and compassion. We have the ability to change our actions and behaviors and to make amends. This capacity for self-healing and repairing relationships is a key to overcoming burnout. Regretting my initial compliance, this realization spurred me to redefine my relationship with my manager and strengthened my courage muscles to advocate for my colleagues and team, a challenge I soon faced again.

In the next one-on-one meeting with my manager, I voiced my concerns about an impending organizational change. With all the courage I could summon, I implored her to provide more transparency and precise guidance to the leadership team, who felt lost and uncertain.

I vividly remember her clear gaze and steady voice as she responded, "I know what you need from me, but I won't do it." In the face of my silent disappointment, she firmly reaffirmed her stance, "I just won't." This time I was less surprised but still, with a heavy sigh, I openly conveyed my frustration and left the meeting with my head hung low.

Initially, I felt defeated and frustrated. But eventually, those feelings subsided. What I had failed to grasp was that she had given me a gift. She firmly established a clear boundary and, in doing so, liberated me. It was as if she said, "I understand what you need. But I won't conform to your expectations. The next move is yours."

Upon reflection, I realized I was firmly rooted in a self-righteous mindset, convinced of what our team needed from her. I had overlooked different solutions and didn't extend the empathy and understanding she also deserved in that moment.

Her words catalyzed me to let go of my entrenched righteousness and the unmet expectations that accompanied it. This shift was liberating; it helped me reclaim my sense of agency, significantly alleviating the persistent frustration that is a common precursor to burnout. Regrettably, our relationship did not rebound to its former state of trust, a loss I keenly felt. However, I gradually moved away from imposing my expectations on her. Instead, I began to take ownership of my emotions and needs. This shift marked a significant evolution in how I led my team and myself, impacting my approach from that point onward.

Sometimes you reach a point where you realize that the other person can't embrace what you're offering. I often think about what might have unfolded had I approached her later, armed with love and compassion, instead of both of us retreating to our respective zones of fight or flight.

I've come to understand that it's less about who individuals inherently are and more about who they can be in a specific moment. When managing people, we have to be willing to acknowledge the limitations of what someone, a team or even an entire organization, can absorb.

In my case, my boss couldn't provide the transparency and empathy I had hoped for in that moment. Consequently, it fell upon me to chart a different path.

When I asked myself, "How do I want to show up right now? How can I tap into my best self, regardless of what's been handed to me?" the answer came to me clearly: I deserved a relationship with my leader that would enable me to lead others with compassion and courage. So I began planning my exit.

I'm not advocating for you to disengage and make a swift exit when you run into disagreements with your boss, colleague, or team member. Rather, I'm encouraging you to explore those unique aspects that are core to the leader you want to be, and let them light your way forward.

Embracing Resilience and Growth

What if you let the bumps on the road guide you from the edges to the core of what is calling to you to be a better manager? It is said that Thomas Edison once shared that he never failed, but rather found 10,000 ways that don't work.[39] Inevitably, setbacks and challenges will arise on your managerial journey. Embracing resilience means accepting failures as opportunities for growth and learning. As Brené Brown reminds us, "Vulnerability is not weakness; it is the birthplace of innovation, creativity, and change."[40] By embracing vulnerability and admitting mistakes, you demonstrate authenticity and foster a culture of psychological safety within your team. You can transform setbacks into stepping stones toward success with humility and clarity.

Managers are human beings. They can disappoint us even at their best, and at their worst, they might struggle, messily trying their best. It's not usually about malice; it often comes from a lack of the right skills and knowledge, and sometimes they need some room to breathe, relax, and reflect. The good news is that these challenges are fixable.

Your team and coworkers know that you're a human who occasionally stumbles. And when you embrace your authenticity and emotions while leading, you're sending a clear message to your teams: it's OK for them to do the same. Let's spread trust and leadership with vulnerability and humility. That means having the courage to spill some details about our lives, admit where we need a little polish, actively seek feedback from all directions, and put our chips on the table for change.

To become the manager your team deserves, you must first embark on a journey of self-discovery and self-care. You can create a supportive and empowering work environment by nurturing self-awareness, prioritizing mental and physical health, and mastering the art of managing conflicting expectations. Embrace setbacks as opportunities for growth and approach challenges with humility and clarity. Shed shame, reclaim lost pieces of yourself, and lead with authenticity, compassion, and courage. Remember, as you get right within, you'll become the manager every team deserves.

Let the Sparks Fly: How We Grow

Self-awareness and resilience are vital to finding your best version of being a great manager. Recognizing personal limitations and stress factors, particularly in challenging leadership roles, and adopting "mediocrity" as a self-care strategy can help mitigate burnout. Building a supportive network, a safe haven, and the bravery to seek help is crucial for a manager's success and well-being. Now let's turn to some scripts to help you solidify these new tips, hacks, and systems to reignite your vitality.

Scripts for Managers and Team

Managers:

- "I can tap into my capacity to be my best self no matter what I may be handed."
- "How do I want to show up today for myself and my team?"
- "I will begin my day in a positive tone by tuning into my heart and inner voice, and distinguishing them from the noise that disrupts my peace."
- "I will prioritize fortitude and clarity when making tough choices, and I'll be kind and understanding to myself and others, even when things get messy and demanding."
- "I acknowledge my limitations and am transparent with my team about my capacity."

Teams:

- "I deserve to have a healthy relationship with my manager."
- "I will encourage myself and my coworkers to prioritize their well-being and mental health."
- " I will contribute to an environment where admitting limitations and seeking help is normalized."
- "I seek to create opportunities for coworkers to share their struggles, ideas, and successes."
- " I will emphasize the importance of clarity and shared understanding in sustaining healthy work relationships."

Striving to be our best selves—to be "right within"—is a process, just like preserving our well-being. Continually reflect on your management style, ensuring it's aligned with self-awareness, empathy, and resilience, and watch the sparks fly.

PART
IV Beyond Burnout

8

Beyond Burnout

"I believed that as a Black woman, I was meant to work hard and endure the most. I mistook my suffering and pain as a rite of passage." As an executive helping lead a New York City museum, Madison Utendahl endured a grueling schedule: working seven days a week, ten hours a day.[1] She faced severe pancreatic issues and acne and, despite dietary changes, struggled with extreme fatigue and inflammation, leading to three hospitalizations. A turning point came when her doctor advised her to reevaluate her life, asserting that her health issues were stress-related. "You have nothing wrong with you," he said, "Your issue is stress."

In response, Madison made a bold move: she resigned from her job, took a six-month break to realign her life, and delved into understanding burnout. This exploration became pivotal when she became the founder of Utendahl Creative, where she implemented an innovative anti-burnout policy.

This policy, an agreement all new hires are encouraged to sign, supports organizational structures that combat burnout. It includes no Monday meetings before noon to ease the Sunday Scaries, ending Friday meetings by 2 p.m. for a stress-free transition into the weekend, scheduling only internal meetings on Wednesdays for better week planning, and providing extended breaks—the last two weeks of December, two weeks in August, and Easter.

The outcome has been impressive, with high retention and satisfaction levels within her team. Madison emphasizes that workplace structures often contribute to burnout, noting that while Gen Zers and Millennials sometimes get a bad rap for not having the same work ethic as Gen Xers and Boomers, perhaps they just don't want to be burning to the ground for work. She stands firm against client pushback on her generous time-off policies, viewing it as a chance to reassess the partnership's compatibility. Her stance is unwavering: she will not risk her or her team's health for work.

Madison's tale is a masterclass in unlearning the deeply ingrained culture of overwork and prioritizing well-being structures and practices in the workplace. In this chapter, we're diving into how life throws you off balance and the managerial practices that can get you back on track. Now, you might be scratching your head, thinking, "Hold up, this all sounds amazing, but where do I begin? My life's already spinning on a fiery hamster wheel!"

Well, here's a little ray of sunshine for you: reigniting your joy for leading people doesn't need to be complicated or eat up your precious time. All you need is a set of practical tools and resources in your management toolkit that suit your style and a receptive and open mindset.

Let's go back to the beginning.

The Burnout Cycle

For many of us, Madison's story isn't exactly a newsflash. We're well-versed in the tale of stress gone wrong, yet for some reason we keep playing it down. There's always that one extra project nudging us, or a problem winking for a solution just before we think of hitting the pause button. We tell ourselves, "Let's just power through this week, then we can catch our breath." But, lo and behold, that magical "next week" remains a mythical creature. Excuses and emergencies stack up like a precarious Jenga tower, and "next week" becomes a never-ending loop.

Meanwhile, we end up letting down ourselves and our nearest and dearest. And it's not just about you. Your entire team is careening toward Burnoutville. Here's a sneak peek of what the burnout cycle looks like for most of us:

1. **Bright-Eyed Beginnings:** Ah, the honeymoon phase! Here, your team is like a bunch of superheroes—working absurd hours, skipping those quaint little things called "breaks," and powering through tasks.

It's all high-fives and energy drinks, with everyone seemingly fueled by sheer determination and too much caffeine.

2. **Oops, the Rose-Tinted Glasses Crack:** But wait! Soon enough, our superhero capes start fraying. The unbeatable team begins to show signs of being, well, human. Mistakes start popping up like unannounced visitors, work quality takes a nosedive like a toddler in a stroller who's just had enough, and it seems like everyone's caught the latest bug making the rounds—twice. The office vibe? It's gone from buzzing like a beehive to more of a weary drone.

3. **The Great Burnout Bake-Off:** Finally, we hit the grand finale. It's like a reality TV show where the plot is that everyone's running on empty. Team members hand in resignation letters. The ones left behind juggle more tasks, teetering on the edge of breaking down. People snap at each other. Morale is subterranean. The once mighty team? Now it's more like a band of apathetic zombies.

So there you have it—the epic saga of working oneself to the point of diminishing returns. It starts with a bang but ends with a whimper (and many job vacancies). Let's not forget that people need to be at their best to perform at their best. Sure, it's easy to shrug and say folks take on too much. If you remember nothing else from this book, etch this in your memory: **burnout isn't a solo performance**. It's a full-blown group number—a preventable systemic and social problem.

And fixing the burnout problem isn't something we can do alone, either. It takes responsibility and action.

Leading People Beyond Burnout

If you've hung in there and read up to this point, you're probably nodding along to one or more of these scenarios:

- You're so burnt out that the light at the end of the tunnel seems like an oncoming train.
- You're itching to dial down the exhaustion, the eye-rolling cynicism, and the "why bother" vibe at work, but you feel useless.
- Deep down, you know the makings of a good manager, but your senior leaders are almost *aggressively* uninspiring.

No matter where you are in your management journey, there's one thing you can absolutely be sure of when it comes to leading people: The best approach is the one that's best for *you*. The best strategies are the ones that support you as an individual, with your own unique aspirations, talents, and quirks.

Yes, it's becoming more common to see managers feeling disengaged and dour in their roles. The job is challenging, no doubt. Yet in those I mentor and advise, there's an eagerness to do well and enhance their impact. They want support for both themselves and their teams; they're looking for a breather, *not* a backdoor exit. And because life is messy and unpredictable, you need practices that you can adjust to your shifting, day-to-day needs.

I will share a few practices that can help us move through and beyond burnout. But before that, let's talk about what should happen first.

The Practice Before the Practice

When was the last time you had a heart-to-heart with yourself, unearthing latent wisdom? My hope is that you reignite your zest for work when you need a recharge, and transform your inner world into a well of strength, not just a cozy hideout.

But before we dive into the deep end of the pool, there's a warm-up routine—a bit of reflection that brings us close enough to get a whiff of what we want our work leading people to be about.

The Practice Before the Practice by Mark Nepo delves into various global traditions where the preparation is as significant as the actual work. In Japan, before you can get your hands dirty with clay on the potter's wheel, you've got to be the potter's shadow for years. In Hawaii, would-be sailors first sit on cliffs, staring at the ocean to understand it. In Africa, children gently touch drum skins, imagining the rhythms they will create long before they play. In Vienna, young musical talents visit piano makers to witness the birth of the keys they will one day play. In Switzerland, it's said that master watchmakers sit and soak up the ticking of time sounds before working those tiny gears.[2]

Nepo draws us into this appreciation of the journey by recounting how the legendary cellist Pablo Casals smiled when asked why he continued to practice four hours a day at 92 and said, "Because I think I'm making progress."

This profound, meaningful acknowledgment—a love for the process—not only shields us from burnout but can also transform us into the leaders we want to be.

OK, now we're ready for some practices.

Practice #1: Deepen Your Self-Awareness

"You carry the cure," as Rumi so eloquently put it, is a sentiment that resonates powerfully in leadership.[3] This perspective positions people leaders as decision-makers and wise mentors who unearth and impart insights that heal and enlighten. Our role transcends traditional management; we are nurturers and guides for those we lead. We carry the soul's balm within.

This path, however, isn't without its trials. It can feel isolating, alienating, and sometimes misunderstood. Yet within this solitude lies a profound sense of purpose and dignity. Embracing our role with awe and respect transforms our leadership into an enriching experience of mutual healing and growth.

This approach to leadership requires a heightened level of self-awareness. It involves a continuous process of self-reflection and empathy, understanding our emotions, strengths, and weaknesses, and recognizing how these elements influence those around us. As managers, we embody the cure—not only for our challenges but also for those faced by the people we lead. By fostering this self-awareness, we pave the way for shared growth and enlightenment.

Practice #2: Reframe Your Inner Scripts

Throughout this book, I've shared scripts to help harness thoughts and conquer nagging doubts and fears. Now, taking inspiration from a piece on rewriting inner scripts by the School of Life—an online platform dedicated to promoting tranquility, self-awareness, improved relationships, and fulfillment in various aspects of life—let's turn our focus to the everyday scripts that trip us up at work.[4]

We all tread through life carrying internal storylines shaped by our earliest experiences and deepest fears. Much like prewritten scripts, these

narratives dictate our expectations and reactions, often stemming from the
more difficult chapters of our childhood. Take a look at these familiar scripts:

- When I make a mistake, I brace for severe criticism. So I rarely own
  up to my errors.
- When I trust someone, they often betray me. So I'm always on the
  defensive.
- If I show strong emotional expressions, it might feed into stereotypes
  about my gender, race, or sexual orientation. So I often opt for a
  more reserved demeanor.
- If a colleague overlooks me, I interpret it as a sign of feeling unwanted
  or undervalued. My knee-jerk reaction is to respond with hostility to
  any perceived neglect.

These scripts are not only influenced by our experiences but, regrettably,
often dictate our current workplace interactions. Often, we're unaware of
their deep-rooted influence. They end up impacting how we *experience*
work, leading to opportunities for healthier, more constructive interactions.
A gentle suggestion from a boss can be misconstrued as harsh criticism due
to our ingrained fear of reprimand. A misunderstanding with a coworker
might escalate into a conflict fueled by our past experiences of betrayal.

The solution lies in considering the potential for different, more
positive outcomes:

- Yes, I messed up, but it doesn't automatically warrant harsh criticism.
- Yes, a colleague let me down, but that doesn't mean they lack
  respect for me.
- Feeling overlooked doesn't have to escalate into a full-blown con-
  frontation or resentment.

The first step in moving beyond these constraining narratives is
acknowledging and understanding them, which begins with introspection.
Reflect on statements like:

- When I make a mistake at work. . .
- When I trust a coworker. . .
- If I express emotion in the office. . .

The goal is to approach our professional lives free from the chains of these past narratives, allowing ourselves to react to workplace situations as they are, not through the skewed lens of previous experiences.

Practice #3: Embrace Flow in Chaos

Have you ever caught yourself in a zen-like flow while sorting out your cluttered closet? It's like discovering a secret haven of tranquility.

We're all too familiar with collective fatigue, but I believe that deliberate moments of flow can help avoid burnout. Imagine channeling a state of flow while untangling the emotional clutter at work—the unresolved issues, overwhelming tasks, feelings of impostor syndrome, instances of hostile behavior, and the frustrating lack of acknowledgment. Picture the rejuvenating energy that could surge through your day as you methodically clear out these mental cobwebs.

Consider this: Do you honor your needs and the needs of your team for growth, safety, and dignity? Or do you sideline them?

Here's an example: "When you're burned out, you have to take contrary action. That which scares you and feels the opposite of what you should do," said my friend Nely Galan, an accomplished entrepreneur and former media executive, when we spoke about burnout for women of color. And she speaks from experience.[5]

When Nely was at what many—including her agents and peers—considered her career's peak, she left it all behind to pursue higher education in search of her "true calling." This led her to discover her passion for financial empowerment and cracking the code within her Latino community. "At any moment, you can change your life," she said.

Nely's story highlights the transformative power of stepping back, reassessing, and clearing mental clutter to uncover one's true purpose. This story illustrates that redefining one's path can lead to rediscovering clarity, peace, and flow, emphasizing the transformative potential of personal reflection and change.

What mental clutter could you clear away to fulfill your calling? Sometimes, a pause from work or immersing yourself in a creative project, even briefly, can help refresh and find that much-needed peace and clarity.

Don't underestimate the power of a good laugh when the flow seems elusive. Humor is my not-so-secret weapon, a precious gift passed on from my family, and an incredibly effective stress-buster. I firmly hold to the belief, instilled in me since childhood, that every interaction should be bookended with a smile. This approach isn't just about being pleasant; it's a strategy for resilience. My smile is hard-earned, and I often lean on it to regain my flow.

There are times when the sheer ridiculousness of work situations becomes overwhelming. Finding humor in the chaos is like a breath of fresh air in those moments. It allows me to step back, take a deep breath, and rediscover my flow amid the madness. A hearty chuckle can be the bridge back to my center, helping me navigate through the day with a lighter heart and a clearer mind.

Practice #4 Fuel Your Light

Everyday, we're bombarded with decisions, but how often do we stop and think, "What's gonna light my fire today?" Sure, we get the drill about drawing lines in the sand, not overloading our plates, leaning on friends, and throwing some love our own way. Yet, we often struggle to walk our talk.

Here's the truth: Instead of taking charge of how I want to groove through my day, I often let my calendar seize control. And I even have a knack for squeezing in those last-minute "Can I just get your thoughts on this?" meetings right into the few precious breathing spaces I thought I'd have. Those familiar habits of people-pleasing, workaholism, and constantly racing against the clock push us to say "yes" when we ought to be boldly replying with a firm "no." Sadly, this habit derails both my zen and productivity.

Here are some valuable practices I've gathered from management resources, the guidance of coaches, and my quest to carve out room for things that fuel my energy and joy.

- **Be intentional with your "Yes."** Now, don't get me wrong; "no" is a fabulous word. But let's not kid ourselves; we're all suckers for "yes." What we say "yes" to isn't just a casual nod; it's a VIP pass to your time, energy, and focus. So, think twice before you say "yes" to that time-sucking meeting or agree to sponsor another project.

The VIP "yeses" are the ones that align with your strengths and expertise, fit your role, make a difference, and bring you alive. Before answering a request, pause and reflect by asking yourself these questions:

- Is this the best and highest use of my time?
- Do I have bandwidth to deliver on this commitment?
- Will saying "yes" contribute to my most important and time-sensitive work?
- Is this person's urgency my responsibility or can I refer them to a better resource?
- Am I saying yes because I feel that I still need to earn my place? And is that true?

Whether agreeing to a meeting or taking on an extra project, every "yes" consumes our time, energy, and focus. The juiciest "yeses" are those that light you up.

- **Trade-offs and Priority Remix:** I've told you I love scripts, and now I'm going to tell you why: I'm an introvert wrapped in an extrovert's costume. Yep! I write more drafts than a writer on deadline, and I've got scripts for days. Why? I'm more inclined to be snuggled up in bed than mingling at a networking event. Yet I firmly believe that even the lightest, most casual conversation deserves meaningful attention.

When in doubt, scripts are my go-to. They help me organize my thoughts, banish nagging doubts, and build my confidence. Plus, they keep me from blurting out "yes" when I should be saying "no, thanks!"

So when you're feeling the pressure to please or prove at the expense of your workload and peace of mind, consider grounding yourself with these:

- "Thank you for thinking of my team. Let me review their capacity against current priorities and get back to you in a few days."
- "Whoa, that opportunity sounds exciting, I'm flattered you considered me. Currently, I'm fully immersed in a project, so I need to discuss it with my manager before considering anything new."

It's hard to say no to your boss when they drop that latest cool project on your lap. This is not a time to be shy about the resources and energy it'll devour in execution. Saying "yes" when your plate is already heaping is like ordering dessert after a five-course meal—trade-offs are involved. So gather your team and have a heart-to-heart about timelines, workload, quality, and, most importantly, peace of mind.

Here are script recommendations for those moments:

- "To make room for X, Y might need to be postponed. Does everyone understand and agree with this change?" (For extra wisdom on handling these trade-offs like a champ, check out the Management Center's "Managing Through Uncertainty: Strategies for Middle Managers."[6]
- "I can deliver an MVP (minimal viable product) version of X by next week, but if we're aiming for a go-to-market version, I'll need at least four weeks. Would that meet your goals?" (For the lowdown on the "gold star" versus "good enough" deal, give the Management Center's "How to Actually Reprioritize" a read.)[7]

By embracing these practices, you can flip that management mindset from "burnout central" to "lit central." It's all about creating a work life full of vibrancy and satisfaction.

Practice #5: Be Radically Human

Korn Ferry's exploration of the "radically human" concept underscores a revolutionary way of rethinking organizational operations.[8] It advocates for a heightened emphasis on valuing individuals, adapting to change, clarifying purpose, and encouraging innovation. This approach redefines traditional operational models, making them more responsive, human-centric, and attuned to the evolving needs of both employees and the wider stakeholder community.

I always remember a valuable lesson from a former boss who stressed the importance of not forgetting the "human" element in human resources. This was crucial during challenging tasks like layoffs or interactions with difficult leaders. I valued that reminder then and have echoed it to my teams repeatedly. Being radically human means safeguarding our core human traits in a corporate world that might otherwise diminish them.

Embracing a radically human approach can mitigate workplace stress and curb burnout, nurturing a culture of empathy, compassion, and shared understanding. To guide this shift, Korn Ferry suggests asking:

- Are we being bold enough in our ambition and innovation and humble enough to learn from our failures?
- Do our people truly understand what our customers want, and are they relentlessly pursuing those goals?
- What would need to change to fully unleash the power of our people? What would being radically human mean for us?
- What beliefs are we going to need to overcome to change the way we do business?
- If not me, now, then who, when?

Consider these questions as gentle nudges to reignite the habits and attitudes that allow us to bring out the best in each other. Start with one or two, and watch what happens.

Practice #6: Build Your Personal Pharmacy

Understanding when to take a mental health day or seek professional help is vital in today's demanding leadership landscape. The rigors of modern leadership don't just challenge our minds; they impact our physical health. Studies have shown that leaders who incorporate mindfulness practices into their routines experience reduced stress levels, improved decision-making abilities, and an overall enhancement in well-being.[9]

Wellness coach Marguerite Clark once highlighted an insightful concept: on our journey toward better mental and physical health, we essentially create our own pharmacy.[10] Reflect on the activities that help you alleviate stress. Why aren't these a regular part of your routine? What are the skills or "muscles" you need to develop on your health journey? Often, it's the small daily rituals that make a significant difference: How you start your mornings, how you talk to yourself, what you choose to read, the content you watch, the people you spend your energy on, and what and who you allow into your personal space. Cumulatively, these small decisions form the essential tools in your resilience-building pharmacy.

Key to this self-care regimen are regular physical activity, a nutritious diet, and dedicating time for relaxation and introspection. These practices not only refresh our minds but also bolster our leadership abilities.

Normalize mental health and well-being. People respond to traumatic experiences in diverse ways. Life events like the loss of a loved one, divorce, severe injury, military combat exposure, sexual assault, domestic violence, or other demanding professional, familial, or personal situations can lead to a range of emotional responses, from grief to depression. Mental health counseling and treatment play a pivotal role in providing support not just for those who have undergone such experiences but also for individuals grappling with other mental health issues. Diving into mental health care for your wellness and recovery isn't just good for you—it's good for your entire team.

Proactive management of mental health conditions is a vital part of supporting both individual wellness and team recovery. Remember, people with mental health conditions can *and do* perform their responsibilities competently every day. If you or someone on your team needs professional help, seek it.

Practice #7: Release Shame

Ever caught yourself in a loop, replaying "what ifs" and "if onlys"? Dwelling on past slip-ups and missed shots can weave a persistent web of shame that's tough to shake off.

I endured the scorching heat and suffocating smoke while leading people through tumultuous times before I finally discovered the right tools, support, and courage to be there for both myself and my teams. These experiences are what inspired me to write this book—to help other people managers delve into the aspects we often avoid out of fear and shame—the broken elements, the issues we ignore, the areas of complacency, and the fears leading to our unraveling as managers.

Life's a canvas of choices—do we see boulders blocking our path or stepping stones to what lies ahead?

Even as we look ahead with optimism, we're still on the road, not quite at our destination (which is less important, anyhow!). This in-between stage, this transitional phase, can feel like a rough tightrope walk. Yet this is where we can cultivate the bravery and inventiveness needed for the next chapter. What lies ahead? Who knows! That's a story we're all writing together.

Shedding the weight of shame allows us to rediscover our true selves and confront challenges with clarity. This journey is more than just bouncing back from lows; it's an evolution into the kind of leader we yearn to become—resilient, empathetic, insightful, and deeply attuned to our needs *and* those of the people we lead.

Beyond Burnout

"Once you know the bad place, you don't go back." Jennifer Bahrami's journey as a social impact executive and a "third culture kid" highlights the complexities of cultural identity and career intertwining, leading to burnout.[11]

Growing up in Peru and South America but feeling disconnected to her dual US-UK nationality, she grappled with her identity beyond her professional roles. Despite achieving success, she lacked a sense of belonging, community, and joy, often wondering about her self-identity. As she put it, "If Jennifer is not representing a CEO or brand and is not from a special country or place, then who is Jennifer?"

Jennifer thought if she kept achieving professionally and was recognized with leadership roles, she could find something she needed to see in herself. Instead, she kept finding herself in toxic work situations. With each climb up the ladder, she felt empty and exhausted instead of successful. Once she took six months to reassess her life and career, including engaging with a career coach, she took control of her narrative and choices. Jennifer now leads a thriving social impact and brand consultancy where she feels creative, joyful, and able to control her days to benefit herself and her family.

Jennifer's story reflects the stories of many women who burn themselves to a crisp on workplace treadmills not designed for them. In our conversation, she poignantly asked, "When you don't have privilege, how do you get lit up?" This question resonates with my guilt for having the opportunity to project-manage my wellness journey, including writing this book.

As another senior Latina executive put it, "Integrity is expensive."

This statement echoes the high cost of maintaining integrity in the workplace. It serves as a reminder of how the enticing allure of professional success, often symbolized by "golden handcuffs," can lead to burnout. This executive's insight captures the essence of many professionals' struggles: balancing personal values with the demands of a high-pressure work environment.

This Latina leader went on to share her admiration for my decision to leave the corporate world. Her vulnerability was palpable as she sought my guidance to chart her exit. Despite her high-ranking position, her professional life had become a source of profound discontent. She led crucial change management initiatives, yet faced a daunting reality: a pervasive resistance to change. Her colleagues, ill-equipped and reluctant to adapt, struggled in a corporate culture marred by interpersonal conflicts and political strife. Her efforts to reform an emotionally charged HR system while pushing for racial equity hit a wall of resistance—the organization's refusal to embrace transformation led to financial losses and team burnout.

"In our pursuit of change, we failed," she confessed. "Now we're turning to external solutions." This shift only deepened her team's frustration and exhaustion.

I've been in her shoes before. I've felt worn down trying to implement change in organizations resistant to it. I've struggled to build understanding with leaders and coworkers whose aspirations, incentives and perspectives differed from mine. I've also found myself trapped by the allure of stability and financial security, staying in roles leading to burnout and missing the signs that could help me and my teams. Change is never easy. Yet these trying moments often guide us to where we need to be.

As I've learned, burnout isn't just an occasional hurdle; it's a persistent, shape-shifting condition that demands a more dynamic and connected leadership.

We're steering through an unprecedented era of global and internal organizational turmoil, marked by slowing economies, rapid technological advancements, shrinking budgets, escalating emotional tensions, and leaders often trapped in ideological crossfires. In this landscape of volatility and uncertainty, the true power of leadership lies in nurturing a sense of direction and community. After all, when our team thrives, everyone thrives.

Getting there requires tapping into a more profound sense of connection and a spirit of collaboration, where shared understanding, support, and teamwork are essential components. It's about harnessing the collective spark and channeling it toward shared ambitions. For managers, it's less about command and control and more about guiding and helping our teams explore and find their collective why. Without these shared experiences and mutually supportive relationships, we risk succumbing to burnout.

Maya Angelou's insight becomes even more pertinent during these turbulent times: "Do the best you can until you know better. Then, when you know better, do better."[12] As managers, our path is fraught with emotional and at times physical demands. We must lead empathically, uphold integrity, and commit to continuous growth and self-improvement. We can prioritize our moral compass and well-being over external pressures and short-term financial gains. Our true test is to rise above burnout, learn from it, and savor the moments when you feel most vibrant and alive.

Challenging the status quo and breaking away from conventional paths is daunting but essential in overcoming burnout and reigniting our joy in leading. Sometimes, we must act on faith, hoping our efforts are worthwhile; and, occasionally, we're lucky enough to witness tangible results of our efforts. My passion for leading people is fueled by a belief in the transformations that happen when people seek understanding. Witnessing the healing and growth in those I've had the privilege of leading humbles me and continually enriches my understanding.

I've learned that we are capable of far more than we imagine. I've seen colleagues and team members flourish, driven by their belief in themselves and the support of others. It's important to remember that we're not in this alone; together, we can make workplaces work for *everyone*.

Management is more than a role—it's a calling. It's a practice that invites us to embrace compassion, expansive thinking, and courage, even when faced with limitations and resistance. Identifying those elements of leadership that light us up is the practice that calls us over and over again. This approach shifts our focus from merely recovering from burnout to reigniting the joy of leading people.

Notes

Chapter 1: Where There's Smoke, There's Fire: Recognizing the Signs of Burnout

1. Kelly, Jennifer F., and Helen L. Coons, PhD, ABPP, "Stress won't go away? Maybe you are suffering from chronic stress," American Psychology Association, November 1, 2022.
2. Maslach, Christina, and Michael P. Leiter, "How to Measure Burnout Accurately and Ethically," *Harvard Business Review*, March 19, 2021.
3. World Health Organization, "Burnout an 'occupational phenomenon': International Classification of Diseases," 2019, https://www.who.int/news/item/28-05-2019-burn-out-an-occupational-phenomenon-international-classification-of-diseases
4. Cait Donovan, video interview, October 11, 2023.
5. World Health Organization, "Burnout."
6. Heitmann, Blair, "Your Guide to Winning @Work: Decoding the Sunday Scaries," LinkedIn blog, September 28, 2018.
7. Hess, AJ, "It's not just you. Your Sunday Scaries are getting worse," Fast Company, February 26, 2023.
8. Heitman, Blair, "How To Overcome The "Sunday Scaries," LinkedIn News, June 29, 2022, https://www.linkedin.com/pulse/how-overcome-sunday-scaries-get-ahead-by-linkedin-news/
9. Hess, "It's not just you."
10. Maslach, Christina, and Michael P. Leiter "Understanding the burnout experience: recent research and its implications for psychiatry," *World*

Psychiatry 15, no. 2 (June 2016): 103–111. PMCID: PMC4911781 PMID: 27265691

11. Albieri, Denise, Jodas Salvagioni, Francine Nesello Melanda, Arthus Eumann Mesas, Alberto Durán González, Flávia Lopes Gabani, Selma Maffei de Andrade, and Jacobus P. van Wouwe, "Physical, psychological and occupational consequences of job burnout: A systematic review of prospective studies," *PLoS One* 12, no. 10 (2017): e0185781. doi: 10.1371/journal.pone.0185781. PMCID: PMC5627926. PMID: 28977041.

12. Salvagioni, D.A.J., F.N. Melanda, A.E. Mesas, A.D. González, F.L. Gabani, and S.M. Andrade, "Physical, Psychological and Occupational Consequences of Job Burnout: A Systematic Review of Prospective Studies," *PLoS ONE* 12, no. 10 (2017): e0185781.

13. Maslach, Christina, and Michael Leiter, *The Burnout Challenge: Managing People's Relationships with Their Jobs* (Harvard University Press, 2022).

14. Maslach, C., W.B. Shaufel, and M.P. Letter, "Job Burnout," *Annual Reviews of Psychology* 52 (2001): 397–422.

15. Donovan, Cate, "Burnout Factors: A Holistic View," LinkedIn, September 8, 2022.

16. Gallup, "State of the Global Workplace 2023 Report: The Voice of the World's Employees."

17. Wigert, Ben, and Heather Barrett, "The Manager Squeeze: How the New Workplace Is Testing Team Leaders," Gallup, September 6, 2023.

18. Ibid.

19. Gottlieb-Cohen, Sarah, "The Toll of Workplace Anxiety and What to do About It," Humu, February 27, 2023, https://www.humu.com/blog/the-toll-of-workplace-anxiety-and-what-to-do-about-it

20. Gallup, "State of the Global Workplace 2023 Report."

21. Gallup, "Prevent and Overcome Burnout: A Strengths-Based Guide," 2023.

22. Searle, B.J., J.C. Auton, and S.D. Brown, "The Role of Control in Predicting Depersonalization in the Burnout Process," *Organizational Behavior and Human Decision Processes* 151 (2019): 8–16.

23. Wang, X., L. Liu, F. Zou, J. Hao, H. Wu, and L. Yu, "Sleep Quality, Burnout, and Their Impact on Work Performance among Chinese Nurses: A Cross-Sectional Study, *Journal of Applied Psychology* 50, no. 8 (2020): 887–896.

24. Indeed Editorial Team, "What Are the Benefits of Flexible Work Schedules?" February 27, 2023.

25. Wilding, Melody, "Setting Boundaries: Why, When, and How," *Harvard Business Review*, April 19, 2022.

26. Sanok, Joe, "A Guide to Setting Better Boundaries," *Harvard Business Review*, April 14, 2022.

27. Humu, "State of the Manager Report, 2022."

28. Wigert, Ben, and Sangeeta Agrawal, "Employee Burnout, Part 1: The 5 Main Causes," Gallup Workplace, July 12, 2018.

29. Hersey, Tricia, *Rest Is Resistance: A Manifesto* (Hachette Book Group, 2022).

30. Kalita, S. Mitra, "How to End the Unfairness of Invisible Work," *Time*, September 26, 2023.

Chapter 2: Show Up: Managing Multiple Fires

1. Winfrey, Oprah, *What I Know for Sure* (Flatiron Books, 2014).

2. Bursztynsky, Jessica, "How Cruise Went from Buzzy Self-driving Startup to 'Public Safety Risk,'" Fast Company, December 18, 2023.

3. *The Morning Show*, "Update Your Priors," Season 3, Episode 9, November 1, 2023.

4. Auger-Domínguez, Daisy. "How to Proactively Defuse Tension on Your Team," *Harvard Business Review*, June 13, 2013.

5. Lebowitz, Shana, Marguerite Ward, Rebecca Knight, and Alexandra York, "Here's a List of Major Companies Requiring Employees to Return to the Office," Business Insider, July 19, 2023.

6. Pringle, Eleanor, "Amazon CEO Andy Jassy's Brutal Message to Remote Workers Refusing to Come Back to the Office: 'It's probably not going to work out for you,'" August 29, 2023, *Fortune*, https://fortune.com/2023/08/29/amazon-ceo-andy-jassy-return-to-office-mandate-or-face-consequences/

7. Lean In and McKinsey & Company, "2023 Women in the Workplace Report."

8. Flex+Strategy Group Research Report, "The Now And Next Of Work," 2023.

9. Conference Board, "Survey: 73% of Companies Struggle to Get Workers Back to the Office," PR NewsWire, August 2023.

10. Wigert, Ben, and Sangeeta Agrawal, "Returning to the Office: The Current, Preferred and Future State of Remote Work," Gallup, August 31, 2022.

Chapter 3: The Hulk with Heart: Holding People (and Yourself) Through Rage

1. Tang, Audrey, "A Simple Affirmation to Avoid Self-Righteousness," March 1, 2021, blog, https://www.draudreyt.com/post/a-simple-affirmation-to-avoid-self-righteousness
2. Manning, Katharine, "We Need Trauma-Informed Workplaces," *Harvard Business Review*, March 31, 2022.
3. Grant, Adam, "That Numbness You're Feeling? There's a Word for It," *New York Times*, January 1, 2024.
4. "Compassion Fatigue," *Psychology Today*, https://www.psychologytoday.com/us/basics/compassion-fatigue#:~:text=Those%20who%20regularly%20experience%20vicarious,and%20difficulties%20with%20personal%20relationships
5. Cosio, D., and A. Demyan, "Post-COVID Compassion Fatigue and Loss of Empathy in Healthcare," *Pract Pain Manag* 22, no. 6 (November–December 2022).
6. Neff, Kristin, Self-Compassion Test, https://self-compassion.org/self-compassion-test/
7. Compassion Fatigue Awareness Project.
8. Spring Health, Calm, Headspace platforms.
9. PTSD: National Center for PTSD, https://www.ptsd.va.gov/understand/types/racial_trauma.asp
10. Eyal, Maytal, "Self-Silencing Is Making Women Sick," *Time*, October 3, 2023.
11. Presentation by Megan Duelks at Seramount "WorkBeyond" Summit, New York City, October 18, 2023.
12. Severs, L.J., E. Vlemincx, and J.M. Ramirez, "The psychophysiology of the sigh: I: The sigh from the physiological perspective," *Biol Psychol* 170 (April 2022): 108313. doi: 10.1016/j.biopsycho.2022.108313. Epub 2022 Mar 11. PMID: 35288214; PMCID: PMC9204854.
13. Balban, M.Y., E. Neri, M.M. Kogon, L. Weed, B. Nouriani, B. Jo, G. Holl, J.M. Zeitzer, D. Spiegel, and A.D. Huberman, "Brief structured respiration practices enhance mood and reduce physiological arousal," *Cell Rep Med* 4, no. 1 (January 17, 2023): 100895, doi:10.1016/j.xcrm.2022.100895. Epub 2023 Jan 10. PMID: 36630953; PMCID: PMC9873947.

14. John, Denise, "Sighing Is an Effective Breathwork Technique, According to Researchers." Goop. November 30, 2023. https://goop.com/wellness/mindfulness/cyclic-sighing-breathwork-technique/?ref=new sletter&nlptrk=Story1-Be-Wellness-breathworktechnique&utm_source=Iterable&utm_medium=email&utm_campaign=20231130-newsletter-thursday-shopper
15. Collins, Jim, *Good to Great* (Harper Business, 2001).
16. Aaker, Jennifer, and Naomi Bagdonas, *Humor, Seriously: Why Humor Is a Secret Weapon in Business and Life (And how anyone can harness it. Even you.)* (Crown Currency, 2021).
17. CharterWorks, Book Briefing, February 5, 2021.

Chapter 4: Real Talk: Release Your Hungry Ghost

1. Lorde, Audre, *Sister Outsider: Essays and Speeches* (Trumansburg, NY: Crossing Press 1984).
2. Lion's Roar Staff, "What are Hungry Ghosts?" August 27, 2020. https://www.lionsroar.com/what-are-hungry-ghosts/
3. Armstrong Miyao, Annie, "How to Let Go (When There's Always More to Do), Goop, November 16, 2023.
4. Brooks, Arthur C., "Keep a Failure Journal," Tim Ferriss Show #shorts, YouTube, https://www.youtube.com/watch?v=ksNrJgylX2c
5. Conversation with Rha Goddess, January 12, 2024.
6. Lakshmin, Pooja, *Real Self-Care* (Penguin Random House, 2023).
7. Daminger, Allison, "The Cognitive Dimension of Household Labor," *American Sociological Review* 84, no. 4 (July 9, 2019), journals.sagepub.com/doi/10.1177/00003122419859007.
8. Steindl-Rast, David, "Want to be Happy? Be Grateful," TED Global, June 2013.
9. "Giving Thanks Can Make You Happier," Harvard Health Publishing, August 14, 2021, https://www.health.harvard.edu/healthbeat/giving-thanks-can-make-you-happier
10. Conversation with Zander Grashow, June 2018.
11. BetterUp CHRO Retreat, October 2023.
12. Datu Wellness Retreat, Tuscany, November 2023.
13. Ibid.

14. Pisharod, Sanjay, *Dr. Acharya Vagbhata's Astanga Hrdayam Vol-1: The Essence of Ayurveda* (Ashtanga Hridayam Series), May 24, 2016.

15. Maslach, Christina, and Michael P. Leiter, *The Burnout Challenge: Managing People's Relationships with Their Jobs* (Harvard University Press, 2022).

16. Le Pertel, Noémie, "When Your Employee Tells You They're Burned Out," *Harvard Business Review*, May 10, 2023.

17. Purushothaman, Deepa, *The First, the Few, the Only* (Harper Business, 2022).

18. Berlin Cameron and Benenson Strategy Group, "The Cost of Loneliness: Women, Work & The Invisible Force That's Undermining Them As They Rise," TheL.ist, February 2023.

Chapter 5: Hang in There: Leading Through the Diversity, Equity, Inclusion, and Belonging Firestorm

1. English, Jeanell, "Former Oscars Diversity Chief on 'Micro-and Macro-Aggressions' That Led to Exit," *LA Times*, October 17, 2023.

2. Ogorchukwu Iyamah, Jacquelyn, *Racial Wellness* (Crown Publishing Group, 2023).

3. Reggie Butler, executive training session at Vice, February 2021.

4. Fani, Negar, and Nathaniel Harnett, "Racism Produces Subtle Brain Changes That Lead to Increased Disease Risk in Black Populations," The Conversation, December 15, 2023.

5. Godoy, Jody, "US Court Upholds Nasdaq Board Diversity Rule," Reuters, October 18, 2023, https://www.reuters.com/sustainability/boards-policy-regulation/us-court-upholds-nasdaq-board-diversity-rule-2023-10-18/?utm_source=DO+NOT+EMAIL+-+Full+list&utm_campaign=0fb944690a-EMAIL_CAMPAIGN_2023_10_23_08_22&utm_medium=email&utm_term=0_-0fb944690a-%5BLIST_EMAIL_ID%5D

6. Ryan, M.K. and Haslam, S.A. (2005), The Glass Cliff: Evidence that Women are Over-Represented in Precarious Leadership Positions. *British Journal of Management*, 16: 81-90. https://doi.org/10.1111/j.1467-8551.2005.00433.x

7. Dr. Cindy Pace, LinkedIn post, November 16, 2023.

8. Auger-Domínguez, Daisy, "When Your Efforts to Be Inclusive Misfire," *Harvard Business Review*, May 3, 2022.

9. Sussman, Sally, *Breaking Through: Communicating to Open Minds, Move Hearts, and Change the World* (Harvard Business Review Press, 2023).

10. Adam Grant, social media post, September 17, 2023, https://twitter.com/AdamMGrant/status/1703427240178958586

11. Yoshino, Kenji *Covering: The Hidden Assault on Our Civil Rights* (New York: Random House Inc., 2006).

12. Daisy Auger-Domínguez, various posts and speeches.

13. Yoshino, Kenyi, and Dr. Christie Smith, "Uncovering Talent: A New Model of Inclusion," Deloitte Development, 2013.

14. Stephane, Joane, Heather McBride Leef, Sameen Affaf, Kenyi Yoshino, and David Glasgow, "Uncovering Culture: A Call to Action for Leaders," Deloitte, 2023, https://www2.deloitte.com/content/dam/Deloitte/us/Documents/about-deloitte/dei/us-uncovering-culture-a-call-to-action-for-leaders.pdf?dl=1

15. Daisy Auger-Domínguez, various posts and speeches.

Chapter 6: Find Awe at Work: How to Turn Your Work Nightmares into Epic Adventures

1. Suzuki, Shunryu, *Zen Mind, Beginner's Mind: 50th Anniversary Edition* (Shambhala, 2020).

2. "4Mind4Body: Work-Life Balance," Mental Health America, https://mhanational.org/4mind4body-work-life-balance

3. Haar, J. M., M. Russo, A. Suñe, and A. Ollier-Malaterre, A. "Outcomes of work–life balance on job satisfaction, life satisfaction and mental health: A study across seven cultures," *Journal of Vocational Behavior* 85 no. 3 (2014): 361–373. https://doi.org/10.1016/j.jvb.2014.08.010

4. Evans, Lisa, "Why You Need To Actually Talk To Your Coworkers Face To Face," Fast Company, October 13, 2014.

5. Sutton, Anna, "Living the good life: A meta-analysis of authenticity, well-being and engagement," School of Psychology, Faculty of Arts and Social Sciences, University of Waikato, Hamilton 3240, New Zealand, October 30, 2019.

6. Simon Sinek, X post, June 23, 2021.

7. *R. O. G* Podcast, Episode156, "Daisy Auger-Domínguez—Leading with Humanity: Guide to Modern Management," Host: Shannon Cassidy, November 28, 2023.

8. McPherson, Susan, *The Lost Art of Connecting: The Gather, Ask, Do Method for Building Meaningful Business Relationships* (McGraw Hill, 2021).

9. Kruger, Allison, "That Meeting Was Too Long (and It Probably Could've Been an Email)," *New York Times,* April 10, 2023.

10. Rogelberg, Steven G., "The Surprising Science Behind Successful Remote Meetings," *MIT Sloan Management Review,* May 21, 2020.

11. Darrisaw, Angelina, C-Suite Coach Advisor Meeting, November 13, 2023.

12. Lemek, Stephanie, "The Relationship Between Trauma and Burnout," Medium, July 6, 2023, https://medium.com/hlwf-healthcare-healthtech-lifesciences-wellness/the-relationship-between-trauma-burnout-11e77a679134#:~:text=Work%20environments%20may%20contain%20triggers,levels%20and%20vulnerability%20to%20burnout

13. Charter Pro Interview Transcript, "Conflict-Resolution Skills for Workplace Tension Over the Israel-Hamas War," November 19, 2023, https://deal.town/time/charter-conflict-resolution-skills-for-workplace-tension-over-the-israel-hamas-war-FKVXY67QE

14. Kteily, Nour, and Eli J. Finkel, "Leadership in a Politically Charged Age," *Harvard Business Review,* July–August 2022.

15. Craige Harris, Jason, Facilitator for Planned Parenthood Federation of America and The.List group sessions, January 2023 and November 2023.

16. Mack, Laura, "Restorative Conversations, the Evolution of Difficult Conversations," LinkedIn blog, April 3, 2023, https://www.linkedin.com/pulse/restorative-conversations-evolution-difficult-mack-mba-she-her-/

17. Gallo, Amy, *Getting Along: How to Work with Anyone (Even Difficult People)* (Harvard Business Review Press, 2022).

18. Daisy Auger-Domínguez, LinkedIn post, January 29, 2023.

Chapter 7: Get Right Within: Becoming the Manager Every Team Deserves

1. "Immigrants (We Get The Job Done)," *Hamilton: An American Musical,* Hamilton Mixtape (2016).

2. DeSante, Christopher D., "Working Twice as Hard to Get Half as Far: Race, Work Ethic, and America's Deserving Poor," *American Journal of Political Science* 57, no. 2 (2013): 342–56, JSTOR, http://www.jstor.org/stable/23496601. Accessed 14 Dec. 2023.

3. The Miseducation of Lauryn Hill, "Doo Wop (That Thing), 1998."

4. Gay Griffin, Ada, and Michelle Parkerson, *A Litany for Survival: The Life and Work of Audre Lorde,* documentary film, Third World Newsreel, 1995.

5. Stephanie Nadi Olson, LinkedIn post, November 8, 2023.

6. Gonzalez, Annie, *Flamin' Hot* Premier Panel, Quad Cinema, New York City, June 12, 2023.

7. Serfaty, Sunlen, and Eric Bradner, "Michelle Obama: 'When they go low, we go high,'" CNN, July 26, 2016.

8. Tulshyan, Ruchika, *Inclusion on Purpose: An Intersectional Approach to Creating a Culture of Belonging at Work* (MIT Press, March 1, 2022).

9. Purushothaman, Deepa, *The First, the Few, the Only: How Women of Color Can Redefine Power in Corporate America* (Harper Business, 2022).

10. Daisy Auger-Domínguez, LinkedIn post, June 25, 2023.

11. Goleman, D., *Emotional Intelligence: Why It Can Matter More Than IQ* (Bantam, 1995).

12. Daisy Auger-Domínguez, LinkedIn post, September 7, 2023.

13. Rizvi, Hidayat, "Servant Leadership vs Transactional Leadership: Deciphering Leadership Styles," Servant Leadership, July 6, 2023, https://hidayatrizvi.com/servant-leadership-vs-transactional-leadership/

14. Lancefield, David, and Christina Rangen, "Actions Transformational Leaders Take," *Harvard Business Review,* May 5, 2021.

15. Rizvi, "Servant Leadership."

16. Hunt, Jaime, "Three Management Sins That Could Cost You Your Best Talent," Forbes Communications Council, February 7, 2023, https://www.forbes.com/sites/forbescommunicationscouncil/2023/02/07/three-management-sins-that-could-cost-you-your-best-talent/?sh=73a01e8f38e3

17. Ibid.

18. Maneesh Goyal, shared at Planned Parenthood Federation of America Board of Trustees Practice, launched January 2020.

19. Leah Smart, in conversation with Tim Tamashiro, "In the Arena," September 5, 2023.

20. García, Héctor, and Francesc Miralles, *Ikigai: The Japanese Secret to a Long and Happy Life* (Penguin Life, 2017).

21. Dalton-Smith, Saundra, *Sacred Rest: Recover Your Life, Renew Your Energy, Restore Your Sanity* (FaithWords, 2017).

22. Howard Thurman, https://www.goodreads.com/quotes/6273-don-t-ask-what-the-world-needs-ask-what-makes-you#:~:text=Sign%20Up%20Now-,Don't%20ask%20what%20the%20world%20needs.,people%20who%20have%20come%20alive

23. "The Wholehearted Life: Oprah Talks to Brené Brown," https://www.oprah.com/spirit/brene-brown-interviewed-by-oprah-daring-greatly/all

24. Adam Grant, Thread post, August 17, 2021, https://twitter.com/AdamMGrant/status/1427638140957757455?lang=en

25. Daisy Auger-Domínguez, LinkedIn post, August 16, 2023.

26. Ibid, August 23, 2023.

27. Gallup, "State of the Global Workplace: 2023 Report: The Voice of the World's Employees."

28. Bamboo HR, "The Great Gloom: In 2023, Employees Are Unhappier Than Ever. Why? BambooHR's Employee Happiness Index Benchmarks Employee Satisfaction Across 8 Key Industries," https://www.bamboohr.com/resources/guides/employee-happiness-h1-2023

29. Lorde, Audre, "A Burst of Light and Other Essays Hardcover," Ixla Press, September 13, 2017.

30. Gaskell, Adi, "How Sabbaticals Help Our Careers," *Forbes,* February 27, 2023.

31. Auger-Domínguez, Daisy, excerpts from "Early Lessons From My Radical Sabbatical," WIE Suite Newsletter, Move the Needle, October 5, 2023.

32. Buettner, Dan, "Hara Hachi Bu: Enjoy Food and Lose Weight With This Simple Japanese Phrase," adapted from an article originally published on *Psychology Today,* January 2011, updated December 2018.

33. Bullock, Grace B., "How Your Breath Controls Your Mood and Attention," Mindful.org, September 5, 2019.

34. Seligman, Martin, *Flourish: A Visionary Understanding of Happiness and Well-being* (Simon and Schuster, 2012).

35. Moore, Catherine, and Jo Nash. "How to Practice Self-Compassion: 8 Techniques and Tips," Positive Psychology, June 2, 2019, https://positivepsychology.com/how-to-practice-self-compassion/

36. Sutton, Jeremy, and Jo Nash, "The Self-Care Wheel: Wellness Worksheets, Activities & PDF." Positive Psychology 13, August 2020, https://positivepsychology.com/self-care-wheel/

37. Hamid, Mohsin, https://www.allgreatquotes.com/authors/mohsin-hamid/

38. Svoboda, Elizabeth, "Moral Injury Is An Invisible Epidemic That Affects Millions." *Scientific American,* September 19, 2022, https://www.scientificamerican.com/article/moral-injury-is-an-invisible-epidemic-that-affects-millions/

39. Hendry, Erica R., "7 Epic Fails Brought to You By the Genius Mind of Thomas Edison," *Smithsonian,* November 20, 2013.

40. Brown, Brené. (2010). *The Gifts of Imperfection: Let Go of Who You Think You're Supposed to Be and Embrace Who You Are* (Hazelden Publishing, 2010).

Chapter 8: Beyond Burnout

1. Madison Utendahl, phone interview, December 15, 2023.

2. Mark Nepo, "The Practice Before the Practice," Awakin.org

3. Rumi, "You wake the dead to life," trans. Haleh Liza Gafori, *Poetry Unbound,* December 12, 2022.

4. The School of Life, "Rewriting Our Inner Scripts," December 2023, https://www.theschooloflife.com/article/rewriting-our-inner-scripts/?/&utm_campaign=1566349_December%20Articles%20Email%202&utm_medium=email&utm_source=Campus%20London%20Limited&dm_i=6TU0,XKLP,38HCQH,45IWE,1

5. Nely Galan, video interview, November 13, 2023.

6. Management Center, "Managing Through Uncertainty: Strategies for Middle Managers," https://www.managementcenter.org/resources/managing-through-uncertainty-strategies-for-middle-managers/

7. Management Center, "How to Actually Reprioritize," https://www.managementcenter.org/resources/how-to-actually-reprioritize/

8. Manson-Smith, Laura, Jamie Maxwell-Grant, and Sarah Jensen Clayton, "What Is radically human transformation, and how can you get started?" Korn Ferry, https://www.kornferry.com/insights/featured-topics/organizational-transformation/what-is-radically-human-transformation-and-how-can-you-get-started

9. Hölzel, B.K., et al., "Mindfulness practice leads to increases in regional brain gray matter density," *Psychiatry Research* 191, no. 1 (January 30, 2011): 36-43. doi: 10.1016/j.pscychresns.2010.08.006

10. Marguerite Clark, coaching conversation, October 2023.

11. Jennifer Bahrami, video interview, December 7, 2023.
12. Maya Angelou, https://www.goodreads.com/quotes/7273813-do-the-best-you-can-until-you-know-better-then

Acknowledgments

"If you want to go fast, go alone. If you want to go far, go together."

—African proverb

To my literary agent, Johanna Castillo: Thank you for believing in me from the very beginning, and every day after.

To my partners at Wiley, Leah Zarra and Gabriela Mancuso: Thank you for seeking me out on LinkedIn, believing that I had a story to tell, and for providing a nurturing home for my story to flourish.

To my book coach, my "book whisperer," Bethany Saltman: I couldn't do it without you. My gratitude runs deep for your invaluable advice, deep wisdom, and delightful humor.

To my development editor, Julie Kerr: I'm so grateful we were paired up. Every note and suggestion lit up the work. And to the broader editorial team who made it shine brighter, thank you!

To Phil Clark: Thank you for always responding enthusiastically to my humble requests for your reviews of my work, and helping me elevate everything I put on paper.

To Nicole Johnson, Chee Mee Hu, and Steve Milovich: Thank you for teaching me that it was possible to manage and lead people strategically, expansively, and with heart.

To every person I have had the honor of managing: Thank you for showing me the way, for putting up with my bad jokes, inspiring me to be and do better, caring for me, and offering me grace when I messed up or failed you.

To my fellow managers: Thank you for not allowing the complicated and messy parts of our work, or the fear, uncertainty, disappointment, and fatigue that might come up, to shake your commitment to leading your teams with compassion and courage, all while taking care of your well-being.

To the women in my life who light me up, Alicia Menendez, Ella Bell, Nadja Bellan-White, Charlotte Castillo, Lisa Cowan, Diana Cruz Solash, Elizabeth De León Bhargava, Yrthya Dinzey-Flores, Tiffany Dufu, Erica Gonzalez, Anita Hill, Dominique Jones, Freada Kapor Klein, Lucinda Martinez, Susan McPherson, Cindy Pace, Katy Romero, Reshma Saujani, Carmen Rita Wong, Helene Yan, and the BBRs: I love you.

To the women who agreed to be interviewed for this book, Cait Donovan, Tina Wells, Madison Utendahl, Nelly Galan, and Jennifer Bahrami: Thank you for trusting me with your stories and sharing your hard-earned wisdom.

To those who guided me back to myself and my wellness during my Radical Sabbatical (and beyond), Rha Goddess, Marguerite Clark, Cynthia Gorman, the entire team at Brace Life Studios, the Omega Institute, Datu Wellness, and the Art of Self-Worth: Thank you for caring for my heart, body, and mind with health, strength, and courage.

To my family, Papi (Cachito y Arcadio), Mami, Tia Maritza, Tita Marily, Haydee, Sonny Ray, Legend, Petal, Laksmi, Visnu, Natalia, Brisa, Valentina, Lia, Tia Josefina, Tio Papa, Evangelina, Jose Antonio, Melissa, Uncle Mike y Victor: I am because of you. ¡Los amo!

To Christopher and Emma: *You* are my light. It's all for you. I love you wholly, deeply, and more.

About the Author

Daisy Auger-Domínguez is a forward-thinking global leader and recognized authority on leadership, management, organizational transformations, diversity, equity, and inclusion. Driven by a deep commitment to sharing what she's learned, she wrote *Inclusion Revolution: The Essential Guide to Dismantling Racial Inequity in the Workplace*. Her insights extend to the stage, where her TEDx talk, 'Inclusion Revolution,' outlines a dynamic blueprint for building meaningful and lasting change in the workplace.

Daisy has led human capital practices at Vice Media, Moody's Investors Service, The Walt Disney Company, Google, and Viacom. Her insights have been featured in Harvard Business Review, Forbes, IDEAS.TED, and several leadership books. She has been recognized by Hispanic Executive's Top 10 Leaders, People en Español's 25 Most Powerful Women, the ADCOLOR Legend award, Brooklyn Community Service's Social Impact award, and many others.

Daisy serves on the Board of Trustees at Bucknell University, her alma mater. She lives in Brooklyn, NY, with her husband and daughter.

To learn more about Daisy and her work, visit: daisyauger-dominguez.com

Index

Manning, Katharine, 55–56
Marginalized groups, members of,
    109, 117–119
Market uncertainties, 10, 36–37
Maslach, Christina, 8, 11, 12, 89
McPherson, Susan, 134
Meaningful activities and work, 159, 162
Measured responses, *see* Thoughtful responses
Mediator role, 150
Mediocrity, embracing, 147–149
Meditation, 67, 84–85, 128, 141
Meetings, 83, 130–131, 134–136
Mental clutter, 84–85, 179
Mental health, 86
Mental health conditions, 183, 184
Mental load, *see* Cognitive load
Mental symptoms, of compassion fatigue/
    empathic distress, 57
Mentoring, 130
Microaggressions, 102
Micromanagement, 18
Millennials, 10, 174
Mindfulness practices, 59, 90, 163, 183–184
Mistakes:
    acknowledging, 69, 93
    in DEI work, 101, 112–113
    grace for, 140
    learning from, 77–78, 93, 114, 168–169
    in supportive environments, 114
Modeling behaviors (leading by example), 24,
    112, 120–121
Morning rituals, 148–149
The Morning Show (streaming series), 36
Movement, *see* Exercise

N

Nadi Olson, Stephanie, 151
Naive realism, 138
Nasdaq, 110
National Center for PTSD, 62
Needs:
    communication of your, 80
    conflicts over unmet, 138
    identifying your, 140
    prioritizing needs of others, 5, 55, 80
    self-awareness of, 76
    of teams, in crises, 37–38
Negative events, fixation on, 58

Neglectful Manager archetype, 154
Nepo, Mark, 176
"No," saying, 80

O

Office archetypes, 142–143
Okinawan culture, 163, 164
One-on-one meetings, 22, 83, 90–91
Open-ended questions, 19
Openness, 113
Operational crises, 33–35
Organizational consequences, of burnout,
    11
Organizational reflection, xvii
Organizational restructuring, 5, 56. *See
    also* Layoffs
Overwork, 64

P

Pace, changing, 149
Pace, Cindy, 112
Pain, emotional, 62–64
Painful experiences, 58
Passion, rekindling, *see* Rekindling
    your passion
Passive-Aggressive archetype, 142
Patience, 58
Patrick, Arielle, 153
Pausing, 105, 107, 131, 160–163
People of color. *See also* Women of color
    burnout for, 24–25
    glass cliff for, 111
    supporting, 104
    unequal workplace journeys for, 117, 118
    workplace challenges for, 160
Performative DEI work, 110–111
Permission, asking for, 140
Persistence, 152
Personally, taking letdowns, 53
"Personal pharmacy," 183–184
Pessimist archetype, 142
Pfizer, 115
Physical consequences:
    of burnout, 12, 151, 158–159
    of chronic stress, 6–7
    of racism, 109
    of self-silencing, 63–64
    of stress, 173